BATAVIA PUBLIC LIBRARY DISTRICT

3 617

D0801537

JB
(JOHNSON, LYNDON B.)
     Falkof, Lucille 14.95

Lyndon B. Johnson.

Withdrawn

Batavia Public Library
335 West Wilson
Batavia, Il 60510
879-1393

**Library Charges For
Missing Date Card**

Lyndon B. Johnson

36th President of
the United States

A photographic portrait of Lyndon Baines Johnson taken while he was serving as 36th President of the United States. (Library of Congress.)

Lyndon B. Johnson

36th President of the United States

Lucille Falkof

GARRETT EDUCATIONAL CORPORATION

Cover: *Official presidential portrait of Lyndon B. Johnson by Elizabeth Shoumatoff.* (Copyrighted by the White House Historical Association; photograph by the National Geographic Society.)

Copyright © 1989 by Lucille Falkof

All rights reserved including the right of reproduction in whole or in part in any form without the prior written permission of the publisher. Published by Garrett Educational Corporation, 130 East 13th Street, P.O. Box 1588, Ada, Oklahoma 74820.

Manufactured in the United States of America

Edited and produced by Synthegraphics Corporation

Library of Congress Cataloging in Publication Data

Falkof, Lucille, 1924-
   Lyndon B. Johnson, 36th president of the United States.

   (Presidents of the United States)
   Bibliography: p.
   Includes index.
   Summary: Traces the childhood, education, employment, and political career of the thirty-sixth president of the United States.
   1. Johnson, Lyndon B. (Lyndon Baines), 1908–1973 — Juvenile literature.   2. Presidents — United States — Biography — Juvenile literature.   [1. Johnson, Lyndon B. (Lyndon Baines), 1908–1973.   2. Presidents]   I. Title. II. Title: Lyndon B. Johnson, thirty-sixth president of the United States.   III. Series.
E847.F35   1989   973.923′092′4   [B]   [92]   88-31003
ISBN 0-944483-20-8

91-01145

Contents

Chronology for
Lyndon B. Johnson

1908 Born on August 28 near Stonewall, Texas

1924 Graduated from Johnson City, Texas, High School

1927–
1930 Attended Southwest Texas State Teachers College

1931 Became secretary for Texas Congressman Richard Kleberg

1934 Married Claudia Alta (Lady Bird) Taylor on November 17

1935 Appointed director of the National Youth Administration for the state of Texas

1937 Elected to the U.S. House of Representatives

1941–
1942 Served as lieutenant commander in the U.S. Navy; received Silver Star

1948 Elected to the U.S. Senate

1953 Elected Senate minority leader

1955 Elected Senate majority leader

1961 Became Vice-President of the United States

1963 Assumed presidency on November 22 after assassination of John F. Kennedy

1964 Won landslide election for presidency over Barry Goldwater

1973 Died on January 22 at his ranch in Texas

Chapter 1
Hill Country Boy

Vice-President Lyndon Johnson and his wife, Lady Bird, sat close together in the small, white room at Parkland Hospital. All the shades had been pulled down and silence hung like the sound of death in the air. Was it only less than two hours ago that the President and Mrs. Kennedy had arrived at the airport in Dallas? Jacqueline Kennedy had looked particularly enchanting in a pink suit and matching hat. And how the crowds had cheered and tried to reach out as President John Kennedy's limousine wended its way through the downtown area. Riding several car lengths behind the presidential limousine, Lyndon Johnson, a Texan himself, had been so pleased to see the reception that Kennedy was getting.

Crack! A sharp, distinct explosive noise rang through the air. For a second, even the Secret Service men could not make out whether it was a firecracker, a cherry bomb, or a bullet. And then Kennedy suddenly was falling to his left. Voices yelled commands as the President's car began to speed away.

In Vice-President Johnson's car, a Secret Service agent yelled, "Get down!" He grabbed Johnson's shoulder and pushed him to the floor of the car and then vaulted from the back seat to cover him. The car jerked as it suddenly increased speed and raced to Parkland Hospital.

Now all that was heard from the small group huddled in the hospital room was an occasional whisper or a sigh. Each person was too busy with his own thoughts. The ticking of the clock seemed to get louder with every passing moment. At 1:22 P.M. the door opened. It was Ken O'Donnell, President Kennedy's appointment secretary. Even before the words were spoken, everyone knew from the shattered expression on O'Donnell's face what the news would be.

"He's gone," said O'Donnell. John Fitzgerald Kennedy, 35th President of the United States, was dead at the age of 46, killed by an assassin's bullet.

TAKING CHARGE

Johnson's first thought was that he had to get back to Washington immediately. He had to reassure a nation in shock that the American Constitution provided continuity in government and that there was someone in charge.

However, Mrs. Johnson would not leave the hospital without first seeing Jacqueline Kennedy. She found her sitting alone outside the operating room. With great concern, Lady Bird put her arms around the dazed young woman and murmured, "God help us all."

An hour later, they met again on Air Force One, the presidential plane. The Vice-President had contacted Attorney General Robert Kennedy, the President's brother, who urged Lyndon to take the presidential oath of office immediately. At 2:40 on the afternoon of November 22, 1963, Lyndon Johnson stood before an old friend, Judge Sarah Hughes. On one side of him was Lady Bird. On his other side was Jacqueline Kennedy, her face pale and dazed, her pink suit streaked and caked with her husband's blood.

Lyndon Johnson taking the presidential oath of office on board
Air Force One, *November 22, 1963. Mrs. Johnson is at the*
left; the newly widowed Mrs. Kennedy is at the right. (Lyndon
Baines Johnson Library.)

Immediately after the oath was taken, Lyndon gave his first presidential order: "Rev up the engines. Let's be airborne." The 36th President of the United States, Lyndon Baines Johnson, was on his way to Washington.

ROOTS: TEXAS PIONEERS

The man who flew to Washington on that fateful day was a product of the "Hill Country" in rural Texas. One of Lyndon's biographers would later write, "Without understanding what it meant to grow up in a place like this—no one would ever understand Lyndon Johnson."

The truth about Johnson's early beginnings and his family background is often hard to separate from fiction, for Lyndon Baines Johnson was a master storyteller. In his central Texas accent, he could fascinate a group of people with tales about his family's role in Texas history. He would embellish with vivid details the most ordinary events of his childhood and youth, holding his audience entranced until he had folks laughing or almost in tears. Never mind that many of the stories confused exploits or exaggerated the truth—so much so that biographers have had a difficult time trying to establish the facts about Johnson's family background and his early life.

There was enough truth about Lyndon Johnson's family to have satisfied any red-blooded American boy. The first Johnson of record served in the Revolutionary War. Two of his great-grandfathers, Robert Bunton and Jesse Johnson, settled in central Texas, fought for the South in the Civil War, and both made and lost money raising cattle. But the similarity between them ended there.

The Buntons settled on fertile land and prospered, but the Johnsons settled just beyond them in the Hill Country, where there was limited and erratic rainfall. Originally, the unplowed land, with its hills of tall green grass, seemed to be a settler's delight. In reality, however, the land along the Pedernales River where the Johnsons settled had a few years of abundant crops but many more years of drought.

A Family of Politicians

Both Eliza Bunton Johnson and Sam Ealy Johnson, Lyndon's grandparents, loved to regale their grandson with stories about their frontier experiences. They told him about the days when strong-willed Eliza rode with her husband on long cattle drives and about Comanche Indians who terrorized the Hill Country.

However, Lyndon's father, Sam Johnson, Jr., wanted something more than a farmer's life. Without even a high school diploma, he taught school for three years, but teaching also failed to satisfy him. Finally, he was offered the opportunity to run for election to the Texas House of Representatives and won. Once in the state legislature, Sam Johnson knew he had found his true calling—politics.

Rebekah Baines, Lyndon's mother, came from a distinguished family. Her grandfather had been president of Baylor University, and her father had served in the Texas House of Representatives. When her father died, Rebekah had to work her way through college teaching speech and writing newspaper articles. When she met Sam Johnson, they had little in common except a mutual interest in politics.

After their marriage, Sam brought his bride back to the Pedernales. For the dreamy-eyed, soft-spoken lady who loved poetry, ribbons, and lace, the change was a difficult one. Rebekah was totally unprepared for her role as a housewife in an isolated farm area. And she was forever embarrassed that her first child, Lyndon, was delivered by a midwife rather than by the local doctor, who could not get there in time because of a raging flood on the river.

The willful and pampered young Lyndon Johnson in front of his home. (Lyndon Baines Johnson Library.)

A CURIOUS AND WILLFUL CHILD

Lyndon was born in Stonewall, Texas, on August 27, 1908, the oldest of the five Johnson children. From the very beginning, family members doted on him. Grandmother Baines, who came often to help Rebekah, described her first grandchild as "extraordinary." Grandfather Johnson predicted that he would some day be a United States senator. Little wonder that many people remembered Lyndon as a willful and pampered child, who used clever ploys to gain attention or get his own way.

Lyndon also was very curious. While still a young child, he would run away to visit the one-room schoolhouse down the road. His visits to the school propelled Rebekah to finally ask the teacher, "Miss Kate" Deadrich, to take Lyndon as a pupil. Though not yet five, Lyndon had been taught to read by his mother, but he would refuse to do so at school unless he could sit on Miss Kate's lap.

Although he was the youngest member of the class, Lyndon was regarded with awe, because many of his classmates, some as old as 14, were just now being allowed to go to school by their parents. Years later, after he became President, Lyndon returned to his first school to sign the Elementary and Secondary Education Act of 1965. And with him at the ceremony was his first teacher, Miss Kate.

A Better Education

Because Rebekah was determined to give her children a better education than that provided in Stonewall, the family moved to Johnson City when Lyndon was five years old. Though Johnson City was a county seat, it was a small village of only 300 people, without electricity or a water or sewage system. In later years, Lyndon would describe his youth in Johnson City as that of a "po' boy."

The move to Johnson City seemed to be a good one. For the next few years, fate seemed to smile on Lyndon's family. His father began to do well enough in the real estate business to run again for the Texas legislature. He ran for the legislature six times and never lost an election.

By the time Lyndon was 10 years old, his father was taking him regularly to the sessions in Austin, the state capital. Dressed in a miniature imitation of his father's clothes right down to a Stetson hat, Lyndon would strut down the aisles of the House, copying his father's walk and mannerisms.

The Johnson family home in Johnson City, Texas, about 1915. (Lyndon Baines Johnson Library.)

Both father and son loved to argue, but there was one noticeable difference. Sam wanted to discuss issues; Lyndon wanted to win the debate.

Life Sours Again

Times were changing, however. Prices were falling and Sam's real estate business began to suffer. When Lyndon's grandfather died, Sam decided to buy the ranch on the Pedernales rather than see it broken up. But his timing was terrible. There was a severe drought, the soil had become worn out, and Sam went heavily into debt. By the fall of 1922, Sam had no alternative but to sell the ranch for whatever he could get and move the family back to Johnson City.

Sam's business failures affected the entire family. The only luxury they had was their automobile. For Lyndon, now a tall, scrawny teenager, the family's economic downfall caused a change in his attitude. He rebelled against doing chores, and often refused to do his homework. On those occasions when he had not done his homework, Rebekah would go over his lessons with him as he ate breakfast so he would be prepared for the day's classes.

Johnson City High School consisted of 24 students in three grades, nine through eleven. Lyndon managed to eke out B's in his subjects, often by charming his teachers with his intelligence and speaking ability. He became senior class president and was second highest in the group of six graduates. Although only 16 years old when he graduated, his height and mature manners made him appear older.

California, Here I Come

The only college available to the poor and poorly educated graduates of Lyndon's class was Southwest Texas State Teachers College at San Marcos. Whether Lyndon failed to pass the tests he had to take in order to get into Southwest

Texas or whether he refused to go to college at all is in question. What is known is that after he graduated high school, Lyndon worked shoveling rocks for a new gravel road between Austin and Johnson City. There was little else he was qualified to do, and he hated the work.

One night, after taking his father's car without permission, Lyndon ran it into a ditch and wrecked it. Afraid of what his father would do, Lyndon fled south to the cotton country near Corpus Christi, where he found himself a job working on a cotton gin.

In unbearable heat, with the constant pounding of baling machines roaring in his ears, Lyndon worked 11 hours a day keeping the boiler supplied with wood and water. He let it be known, however, that he wanted to come home, but only if his father did not punish him for wrecking the car. Though Lyndon finally returned home, it was not long before he fled again—this time to California.

Four of Lyndon's older friends had bought an old Model T Ford for $25 and were planning to look for jobs in California, where they heard that jobs and money awaited the ambitious. One of Lyndon's friends had an older brother already living in California who promised to help them find jobs. But when his parents refused to give their permission for him to go, 17-year-old Lyndon ran away while his father was out of town on business.

Lyndon the Lawyer

In later years, Lyndon would talk about the tough life he endured in California, washing dishes, picking grapes—doing any job to survive. In reality, however, when Lyndon reached California he telephoned a cousin, Tom Martin, who was living in San Bernardino. Martin was a successful lawyer whose clients included many famous movie stars. He offered Lyndon and one of his friends a chance to work in his law firm.

Lyndon began to hope that, in time, he himself could

become a lawyer. Though his education at Johnson City High hardly provided the background he needed to pass the California bar examination, he was told that the state of Nevada was more liberal. If Lyndon studied in Martin's office, he could take an oral examination and, with the recommendation of some well-known attorney, be admitted to the Nevada bar. With a Nevada license, California would almost automatically accept him as an attorney.

Lyndon threw himself into his work in a style he had never shown before. He learned to speak with clients on the telephone and to manage the office whenever Martin was absent. He was gaining a whole new world of experience – but no salary. Then, in the summer of 1925, his plans began to fall apart.

After his wife and child left to visit family back in the Hill Country of Texas, Martin went on a wild spree, leaving Lyndon and his friend to handle the office. At first, when clients phoned, Lyndon would call Martin to find out what to tell them. In time, he even began to give legal advice on his own. But as Martin appeared less and less frequently at the office, Lyndon became increasingly desperate. The rent had to be paid, bills were piling up, and he suddenly realized that he could be sent to jail for giving legal advice without a license.

Lyndon also discovered that Nevada had a minimum age of 21 for obtaining a lawyer's license, which meant he would have to spend four years in Martin's office. Furthermore, because Nevada was tightening its standards for entry into the legal profession, Lyndon doubted he would have the necessary qualifications to become an attorney.

Fortunately, Tom Martin's father was driving from Texas to California with Tom's wife and child, and he agreed to take Lyndon back to Texas. Although he had been away from home only 10 months, the experience had taught Lyndon much and had also given him a taste of the good life.

A Time of Comeuppance

Upon Lyndon's return home from California, Rebekah and Sam Johnson hoped that he would now be ready for college, but once again they were disappointed. Lyndon went to work on another road gang, scooping up rocks for two dollars a day. Because he hated the work and his hard life, he rebelled by running with older boys and by playing pranks on other people. To gain attention, he would spend his money on wild shirts, strutting around town and "talking big." "I'm going to be President of the United States," he boasted, causing those who heard him to laugh uproariously.

In the winter of 1927, a new local political administration came into power, and both Sam and Lyndon Johnson lost their jobs. Now, without the security of even a single weekly paycheck, tension in the Johnson family increased. To top it all, Lyndon got into a fist fight.

One night at a dance, Lyndon was dancing with the girlfriend of a husky farmer. Although a sign on the wall clearly stated, "No dancing cheek-to-cheek," Lyndon persisted in snuggling his cheek against that of the young lady. Furious, the young farmer challenged Lyndon to step outside. Though tall, Lyndon was no match for the muscular farmer, who knocked Lyndon to the ground time after time. When Lyndon's friends tried to break up the fight, they were stopped by the farmer's supporters. Lyndon ended up with a bloody face, his fancy shirt blood-stained—and a fine for disorderly conduct!

Now all of Lyndon's arrogance had been pounded out of him. He had fallen as low as he could get. There was no place for him to go—except to college. Within a week, Lyndon was on his way to San Marcos, carrying his belongings in a cardboard suitcase.

Chapter 2
A Better Teacher than Student

outhwest Texas State Teachers College at San Marcos was a "po' boys" school. If in later years Lyndon Johnson distrusted – or envied – those who attended such old, established, eastern universities as Harvard and Yale, his feelings can be understood. For San Marcos, as its students called the school, consisted of only five buildings, including a rickety two-story library.

Because there were no dormitories, students lived and ate their meals in local homes. Since most of the students were products of one-room schoolhouses, the majority of classes were at a high school level. And among the 56 members of the faculty, several had no college degree.

When Lyndon arrived at San Marcos in 1927, he needed a room, a job, and friends. Within a few weeks, he had all three. It seemed that whenever help was needed, a member of Lyndon's family would come through. This time, a young cousin introduced Lyndon to the captain of the football team, who happened to be the most popular man on campus. He invited Lyndon to share the rent-free apartment provided to him as team captain. Shortly after, the president of the student council moved into the same apartment. Suddenly, there was lowly freshman, Lyndon, living with two of the "big men on campus."

It also helped that Lyndon's father had known Cecil Evans, the college president, during Sam's days in the state legislature. Without telling his son, Sam called Evans, who arranged for Lyndon to get a job picking up trash and clearing stones.

Lyndon worked hard to make a friend of President Evans. If the young freshman spied Evans striding across the campus, he would stop his work, approach the president, and chat with him for a few minutes. In a short time, Lyndon found a common link between them—politics! It did not take long for Lyndon to talk himself into an inside job, first mopping the floors of classrooms and corridors and eventually running errands for Evans. Thus, within five weeks after his arrival at San Marcos, Lyndon had created a job for himself as office boy for the college president. He had also doubled his monthly salary from $8.00 to $15.00.

BULL JOHNSON

Yet Lyndon's personality did not endear him to everyone. He could not resist a natural tendency to boast about himself. He told exaggerated stories about the work he did for the college president, about his family history, and about his ability to charm the ladies. He interrupted others when they tried to talk and then proceeded to monopolize (take over) the conversation. Despite his mother's attempts to pass on to her son the elegant manners she had been taught, Lyndon's stabbing and grabbing of food across boardinghouse tables revolted many a fellow diner. In time, he earned the nickname "Bull" Johnson.

The students were also annoyed by the way Lyndon played up to his professors. In informal sessions, Lyndon would sit himself on the ground, looking up at the professor and agreeing with everything he was saying. A day or two later, he might be seen doing the same thing with another teacher, agreeing with *him* — even though the teacher expressed a totally different point of view. Lyndon knew how to flatter people, and he particularly cultivated those in positions of power.

Writing also gave Lyndon an opportunity to build up his self-image. He got a job as an editor on the school paper and eventually became the editor-in-chief. Although his mother wrote his first editorial, Lyndon managed to make sure that his name appeared often in print.

Carol and Cotulla

Once in college, Lyndon was in a great hurry to finish. He stayed at school through the summers so he could quickly get a two-year teaching certificate. By the summer of 1928, Lyndon needed to use that certificate to get a job.

Most students could have lived on the money he was earning, along with student loans and cash presents he received from relatives, but not Lyndon. He could not resist buying clothes that he could ill afford and spending a lot of money on dates. He also bought a Model A Ford for $400, for which payments were often overdue. That summer his money ran out. Lyndon had to get a full-time job.

Each summer, school superintendents would come to San Marcos summer school for seminars. During the summer of 1928, Lyndon became acquainted with the superintendent from Cotulla, a small town in southern Texas. When the superintendent offered Lyndon a job at $125 a month, he jumped at the chance. The understanding was that Lyndon would return to college at the end of the school year.

Romance Enters the Picture

The job at Cotulla seemed doubly inviting to Lyndon because it was within driving distance of Pearsall, Texas, where Carol Davis, a recent graduate of San Marcos, was also teaching. For much of his second year, Lyndon had been courting Carol, who seemed to him to be an ideal prospect for a wife. She was attractive, could help him write term papers, and had her own car. Moreover, her father was a former mayor of San Marcos and one of its most prosperous citizens.

Carol's father, however, was not too keen about the young man from the Hill Country. He is reported to have told his daughter, "I don't want you getting mixed up with those people. That's the reason I moved away from the Hill Country. I wanted better for my children."

While at Cotulla, Lyndon spent many weekends visiting Carol. But she soon began to have as many concerns about the brash young man as her father had. She was interested in music; Lyndon was not. Lyndon was interested in politics; she was not. And when a young man with musical tastes began to appear regularly, Carol began to spend less and less time with Lyndon.

According to Lyndon's version of the breakup of the romance, Carol's father had called Lyndon's grandfather, Sam Ealy Johnson, "nothing but an old cattle rustler." At that, Lyndon had stormed out, sure that the marriage would never work, and leaving Carol in tears.

Whether or not Lyndon was a rejected suitor, by the end of the school year, Carol announced her engagement to her musical boyfriend. Lyndon was to be far more successful that year with his first teaching assignment.

Lyndon Johnson, Teacher

Because Cotulla was only 60 miles north of the Mexican border, most of the town's 3,000 residents were of Mexican descent. Lyndon was assigned to a school in which most of the students were Mexicans. The faculty consisted of five local housewives who arrived just before classes began and left immediately after they ended. As the only male on the faculty, Lyndon was appointed principal, with the additional responsibility of teaching seventh and eighth grades.

Lyndon jumped into the role of teacher with total dedication. He was not interested in his students' culture, but he was vitally interested in them as individuals. Never did those boys and girls from the "wrong" part of town have a teacher who cared so passionately that they learn English.

When Lyndon discovered that the school had no athletic equipment, he quickly talked the school board into providing volleyballs, softballs, and bats. He also got the few Mexican families with cars to provide transportation so his students could participate with other schools in various athletic events as well as in debating contests and spelling bees.

Lyndon's ego was bolstered by the affection showered upon him by the students and their parents. Moreover, his drive, his long hours of hard work, and his demonstration that he cared gave these young people a sense of pride and self-respect that had been missing from their lives. At the end of the year, Lyndon received rave recommendations from the superintendent.

Although it had been a difficult year for Lyndon, he had proven to himself that when he was interested in something, he had an unbelievable capacity for concentration and hard work. He returned to San Marcos in June of 1929 with far greater self-confidence and self-assurance, qualities hard-earned and deserved.

Lyndon Johnson with the 5th-, 6th-, and 7th-grade students of the school where he was a principal in Cotulla, Texas, in 1928. (Lyndon Baines Johnson Library.)

THE CAMPUS POLITICIAN

Once back on campus, Lyndon had two ambitions. He wanted to finish his education as quickly as possible, and he wanted to belong to the popular crowd. Though he had lived with two of its members, the football captain and the student council president, in his first year at San Marcos, Lyndon had never been accepted into their secret organization, called the Black Stars. Although his name had been proposed at one time, he had been turned down.

The members of the secret organization were usually class officers and student council representatives, yet there was a rather half-hearted interest in school politics. There were no burning issues on campus, and school elections aroused little excitement.

In the summer of 1929, a rival campus group, called the White Stars, was formed. It, too, was a secret organization. Lyndon was accepted as a member of the group after his name was proposed by three boys who found his story-telling entertaining.

Once inducted into the White Stars, Lyndon's enthusiasm for politics took over. He talked the members of the new secret club into running an opposition candidate for senior class president. He reminded the White Stars that few students bothered to vote, and if they organized those students who were not Black Stars, the White Stars could win the office. Lyndon knew he had too many enemies on campus to offer himself as a candidate. Instead, he suggested Willard (Bill) Deason, a handsome fellow who was popular with the girls. Lyndon reminded the White Stars that women students made up the majority of the school population.

Lyndon also knew that the campaign needed an issue around which the students could rally. That issue became the "blanket tax," an extracurricular activities fee which all students paid, but which went mainly to support the school's athletic teams. Lyndon argued that a greater portion of the tax should be spent on such activities as debate and drama. The White Stars' slogan became, "Brains Are Just as Important as Brawn."

Day and night, Lyndon collared students, just as his father had done in the Texas legislature. Grabbing them by the lapels, Lyndon would talk to them one by one. The night before the election, however, the White Stars counted noses and decided they were 20 votes short. Lyndon then raced around the campus that night for some last-minute politicking. The next day, Bill Deason won the election.

Rematch: White Stars vs. Black Stars

When the next student council election came up, the Black Stars were determined to win. Politics had now become a hot subject on campus. Because the Black Stars were the most popular group at San Marcos and because they were now stirred up and out to win votes, it looked like the Black Stars would win easily. But Lyndon had another plan up his sleeve.

Many San Marcos students had to leave school temporarily to earn money to continue their education. When they returned to school, it was hard to tell whether a student was a sophomore, junior, or senior because of the different number of courses completed. Taking advantage of this situation, Lyndon advised students voting for White Star candidates to go from one room to another, first voting as a sophomore and then as a junior. If someone challenged a voter in the junior class, the young man or woman shouted, "Don't tell me I'm not a junior. I'm taking more junior subjects than sophomore subjects and that makes me a junior!" Without formal records at hand, it was hard to argue.

Using this strategy, the White Stars won again—and Lyndon was gaining a reputation on campus. Though there were those at San Marcos who would later remember him as the student who stole the election, there is no doubt that Lyndon was learning politics and political strategies. He was also developing a following of loyal admirers who one day would help him form his own political power base in Texas.

Part of this power base would also come from friends Lyndon helped during his time at San Marcos. When Lyndon returned to college after his year at Cotulla, President Evans gave him the task of assigning students to campus jobs. The Great Depression had begun early in the Hill Country. Because cotton and other farm prices had fallen drastically, many students were forced to leave college because they lacked money for tuition. To have a job on campus often meant the difference between getting a college education or returning to work on the family farm. Lyndon knew what to do with his new authority; he gave the best campus jobs to his friends.

LYNDON MAKES A SPEECH

Each summer ever since he was 10 years old, Lyndon had been going with his father to a traditional all-day political rally and barbecue. Hour after hour, the candidates would climb up to the platform, a wagon with its tailgate down, and give speeches. For the folks in south central Texas, this was one of the most important political events of the year.

In the summer before his college graduation, Lyndon and Sam Johnson went to the rally particularly to hear Pat Neff, former governor of Texas who was now running for re-election as the state railroad commissioner. Neff had a reputation for being an excellent orator.

It was almost dark when Pat Neff's name was called by Judge Stubbs, the master of ceremonies. But there was no response. Obviously, Neff had not yet arrived.

"Anyone want to speak for Neff?" the judge called out, but nobody answered. "If no one is willing to say a few words for Neff, we'll just have to move on," said the judge, but still no one spoke.

Sam Johnson could not stand to have Neff's name pass without a word of support. He had worked with the governor years before, and Neff had recently helped him get a job.

"Get up there, son," Sam whispered to Lyndon. "Say something for Pat."

Almost instinctively, Lyndon shouted out, "I'll speak for Pat Neff!" Climbing onto the tailgate of the wagon, Lyndon, bathed only in the light of the barbecue fire, looked over the crowd and began. His enthusiasm and his arguments in support of Neff more than made up for his thin, reedy voice and the overly dramatic speaking gestures he had learned in high school. He spoke only five minutes, but the applause was all Lyndon hoped for. He had made his first political speech. It had come as naturally to him as breathing, and he had found it most satisfying.

Among the candidates who observed Lyndon that evening was Welly K. Hopkins, who was running for state senator. Hopkins was so impressed with Lyndon's arm-swinging speech that he asked Lyndon to help him with his campaign in the two counties Lyndon knew well. Though busy finishing up at college that fall, Lyndon managed to organize a campaign that astounded Hopkins and gave him an overwhelming victory in counties that he figured to win only with a slim margin. For Lyndon Johnson, that spur-of-the-moment speech would open the door to Texas politics and the nation's capital, Washington, D.C.

Debate Coach at Sam Houston High

After Lyndon graduated from San Marcos in the summer of 1930, he once more sought help from a family member. This time it was his Uncle George, chairman of the history department at Sam Houston High School in Houston, Texas. Lyndon begged his uncle to find him a job at Sam Houston High, but there was no opening at the time. Lyndon then contacted the superintendent of schools at Pearsall, whom he had known when Carol Davis had worked there. By September, the Pearsall superintendent had found a position for Lyndon. But after he had been there only a month, his Uncle George called to tell him that there was a vacancy in the speech department at the Sam Houston High School.

The superintendent at Pearsall was stunned when Lyndon notified him he was leaving in the middle of the school year. But Lyndon managed to calm his anger by suggesting his sister, Rebekah, for the job. His sister got the job and Lyndon went to Houston.

A Strict but Popular Teacher

To Lyndon, Sam Houston High seemed enormous. The population of the school, 1,800 students, was twice as large as his college – and the teachers had more advanced degrees than the faculty at San Marcos. But if the young new teacher was overwhelmed by the size of the school and the education of the staff, he never admitted it. When the principal mentioned that the school had never won a city championship in debating, Lyndon, with his usual aplomb, calmly announced, "Don't worry, this will be the year when Sam Houston wins."

Once again, Lyndon proved to be an outstanding teacher. He helped his students overcome their shyness in public speaking by making them all get up in class and produce crazy sounds. Then they began making speeches, first 30 seconds, then a minute, and so on until they were able to make prepared speeches of five minutes or more. One student remembered that he gave an enormous number of assignments, "and he was terribly strict about your doing them."

But the students did not mind, because their teacher made them feel important with his nagging, and he threw himself wholeheartedly into improving each student. Among the students chosen for the debating team were two young men, Luther E. Jones, smart but stiff and aloof, and Gene Latimer, a lad with Irish charm and the gift of gab. (Latimer would eventually serve Johnson for most of his life.) Lyndon worked the two young men tirelessly, long hours after school. He coached their delivery, checked their clothes, and made sure they knew their material. After his team began to win debate after debate, Lyndon visited the editors of the Houston newspapers and soon the team was making news.

Lyndon delivered on his promise: Sam Houston High won the city debating championship that year. Then, after a string of 67 victories, the team went on to the state finals. They made it right to the very last debate, which they then lost by a 2–1 decision. Though dismayed at the decision, Lyndon comforted the two young men, "You did your very best." Then Lyndon went outside and threw up. He was more disappointed than his students.

THE CALL COMES

By his second year at Sam Houston High, there was not enough room for all the students who wanted to be in Lyndon's classes. He had good reason to feel proud of his accomplishments, but he was already looking ahead. Teaching was OK, but politics was his real love. He had been thrilled working with Welly Hopkins, meeting the public, and getting out the votes. He knew he was good at it. Hadn't he come through for the White Stars at college and Welly Hopkins?

And Hopkins had not forgotten. On November 5, 1931, while chatting in the school office, Lyndon was called to the phone. On the line was Richard Kleberg, who had won a seat in the U.S. House of Representatives the day before. Kleberg explained that Welly Hopkins had recommended Lyndon for the job of private secretary to the new congressman. Was he interested?

Lyndon could hardly contain his excitement. Was he interested! With the blessing of his principal, Lyndon left immediately for an interview. Within five days, he was on a train speeding to Washington with Representative Kleberg. His golden opportunity had finally come—and Lyndon Johnson knew exactly what he was going to do with it.

Chapter 3

Learning the Ropes

For Lyndon Johnson's ambitions, Richard Kleberg was the perfect boss. Kleberg had been offered the Democratic nomination because he was well known in Texas and the 14th Congressional District. He was extremely wealthy, being one of the owners of the largest ranches in the state, the fabled King Ranch. He was a sportsman, cared little about business, and was indifferent to politics. The work of the district was left to his private secretary, Lyndon Johnson.

In a letter home, Lyndon described his work day:

Dearest Mother:
    I don't know when I've been so tired as I am tonight. . . .
    To start to tell you how I've worked since I came here would require more time and effort than I feel like expending. I get up at 6 o'clock and go to the office by 7:30, take off 30 minutes sometime during the day for lunch and leave the office about six or seven, depending on the correspondence. I *run* the office *force*. Mr. Kleberg doesn't spend an hour a day there and then only signing letters. Frequently I go back at night to finish so I won't get behind. Am learning fast and doing a good job of my work. The only expressions that Mister Dick has made regarding my work go like this: "Great—Good—That's what I want, etc."

What Lyndon described was really only a small part of his daily activities, for he was determined to learn all the answers—particularly to two questions: "Who had the power?"

and "What is the relationship between these important people?"

Lyndon knew very little about the district Kleberg represented. Yet mail poured in daily from people seeking help from their congressman. Lyndon resolved to answer each letter promptly and solve every problem.

LIFE DURING THE DEPRESSION

It was a critical time for the nation—the third year of the Great Depression. Farm income had dropped so low that a bushel of wheat sold for 25 cents and a bushel of corn for seven cents, which were prices below those of colonial times. Many businesses had failed, and one out of every seven persons was unemployed. People wrote seeking jobs, and veterans of World War I wrote asking for help in getting early payment of bonus money.

The mail seemed never-ending. To stay on top of it, Lyndon brought in the two top debaters from Sam Houston High, Luther Jones and Gene Latimer. Both men, still in their teens, ended up living in Lyndon's room in the basement of the Dodge Hotel so all three could save on expenses.

What Lyndon failed to mention in his letter home to his mother was that he worked Latimer and Jones as hard as he worked himself. All three would put in 18-hour days, often seven days a week. Lyndon would read every piece of mail, make notations on how to answer it, and then give it to one of the young men to type a response. After the daily pile of letters had been completed, Lyndon would go through the district's newspapers and put checkmarks next to articles about such items as a new business, marriages, a Kiwanis Club election, or even high school graduations. He would then make sure that a letter of congratulations was sent.

While Latimer and Jones were typing letters, Lyndon was either telephoning government agencies or rushing out to visit them in order to get answers to all the problems presented in the daily mail. He had come to Washington without any government experience and few political connections, but he had drive, and he knew how to size up people quickly. He also knew how to encourage underlings, and how and when to flatter women clerks and men in power.

Lyndon even took an extra job as doorkeeper on the Democratic side of the House. This gave him a chance to see firsthand the give and take among House members and to study the formal procedures used in running the legislature. He also got to know congressmen and got himself noticed. As one congressional secretary later said, "This skinny boy was as green as anybody but within a few months he knew how to operate in Washington better than some who had been there 20 years."

THE LITTLE CONGRESS

The "Little Congress" was one of the routes that Lyndon used to gain attention in Washington. It was comprised of congressional secretaries. The original purpose of the Little Congress was to get congressmen and senators to come and talk at meetings. This would help the young men get to know everyone on the "Hill," the nickname for the Capitol building area where the Senate and the House of Representatives were. By the time of Lyndon's arrival in Washington, however, meetings of the Little Congress had become dull and membership was falling off. The organization was run much like the real Congress in that its leadership depended on seniority, or how long one had belonged to the club. When Lyndon decided that he wanted to become speaker of the Little

Congress, he used tactics similar to those he had used with the White Stars in college.

The landslide election of Franklin Delano Roosevelt as President in 1932 had brought a whole new group of congressmen and congressional aides to Washington. That provided one cluster of possible voters. As always, Lyndon did his homework and discovered that the club bylaws stated that "any person on the legislative payroll" was eligible for membership. That meant that Capitol Hill mailmen, policemen, and elevator operators also had a vote as long as they paid their two-dollar dues.

Lyndon kept his plan absolutely secret until the last moment. In order to help Gene Latimer earn extra money, Lyndon had gotten him a job as a Capitol Hill mailman, and now Latimer reciprocated the favor by getting as many Capitol Hill employees as he could to join the club. On April 27, 1933, when the meeting of the Little Congress was called to order, the handful of old-timers present were shocked to see a stream of newcomers rushing to take seats. When the votes were counted, the newly elected speaker, Lyndon Baines Johnson, strode to the front of the room to take the gavel.

As speaker, Lyndon delivered exactly what he had promised. Picking up on President Roosevelt's slogan, he offered a "New Deal," and he gave the Little Congress just that. He selected members of the organization to debate issues that were on the floor of Congress. Reporters were invited to attend the debates, knowing the view of a congressional aide could be a clue to how a congressman might vote. Having made sure that the reporters publicized the results of these debates, Lyndon now had a reason for personally visiting important members of Congress and inviting them to speak before the group. Soon congressional legislators became eager to have their future bills debated in the Little Congress, since preparation for the debate, pro and con, helped them to an-

Vice-President John Nance Garner presents a historic gavel, made from a tree planted by Sam Houston, to Lyndon Johnson, speaker of the "Little Congress." (Lyndon Baines Johnson Library.)

ticipate the kind of arguments they might meet on the floor of the real assembly.

Lyndon had turned a dying social club into a dynamic political organization. For him, personally, it meant excuses to meet more of the powerhouses of Congress as well as free publicity for the organization and for himself. Articles in the press about the Little Congress always included a statement from or at least mention of the name of its speaker, Lyndon Johnson.

THE NEW DEAL

Within weeks of taking office as President, Franklin Roosevelt initiated an avalanche of new legislation. There were public works projects offering jobs for the unemployed, help with mortgages for homeowners, and, at last, help for the farmers. The Farm Relief Act, in particular, provided the kind of government action for which farmers had been waiting. Among the reasons for the decline of farm prices was the surplus of farm commodities. Now the government was going to pay farmers *not* to grow corn or cotton or wheat. If they agreed to take some of their land out of production, they would receive government funds. But many farmers were distrustful of government promises and refused to get involved with the confusing "red tape"– the many forms that had to be filled out.

By telephone, Lyndon began an educational program for the farm agents in his district's counties. He explained the Farm Relief Act to the agents and then persuaded them to get farmers in their areas to sign up for the program. Lyndon would then go to work in Washington to see that the applications from the farmers were processed immediately – no easy task. He would telephone a bureaucrat in the Agricultural Adjustment Administration and say, "This is Congressman Kleberg from the Agriculture Committee. I'm sending my secretary, Lyndon Johnson, to see you and I know you'll give him all the assistance you can." When Lyndon arrived, he was able to get prompt action for the constituents of the 14th District.

In July 1933, the first check for plowed-under cotton was presented by President Roosevelt to a farmer of the 14th District. More than 85 percent of the farmers in Kleberg's district signed up for the program, probably the best record of any congressional district in the country.

Setting the Stage for the Next Move

Though pleased with his success, Lyndon was bored with his job as a congressional secretary. He had learned it well; it was now becoming too routine. He was prepared for the next step up the ladder, and his fertile mind was already setting the stage.

Lyndon changed the arrangement of the furniture in Kleberg's office. He moved his desk close to the entrance so that visitors had to speak to him first. Visitors were voters, and Lyndon wanted to be the one who personally handed out passes to the House and Senate visitors' galleries. If the visitor turned out to be important, Lyndon would steer him into the congressman's usually vacant office, sit behind the huge desk, and offer his services.

Letters now going out of Kleberg's office bore Lyndon's signature under a different introduction, which read, "In the Congressman's absence, I am advising you . . ." Even routine information sent to the newspapers bore Lyndon's stamp. If the opening of a new camp for the Civilian Conservation Corps, a government work program, was being announced, the item would begin, "It was announced by Lyndon Johnson, secretary to Congressman Kleberg, that a new CCC camp would be opened at . . ." At Lyndon's suggestion, Kleberg even allowed his secretary to tour his district to meet constituents, including local bankers, newspaper editors, and county party chairmen.

Lyndon was taking on more and more responsibility and authority. He helped secure jobs for friends or influential people back in Texas. He even took the summer of 1934 to assist a fellow Texan, Maury Maverick, win a congressional seat. But unless Kleberg retired or was given an appointed post by the President, there was little chance that Lyndon would find an elective office.

ENTER LADY BIRD

During his early years in Washington, Lyndon had little time for social events. What little social life he did have revolved around his ambitions. At such events as the Texas Society Ball, he danced with the wives of congressmen, hoping to get an introduction to their husbands.

By the summer of 1934, however, Lyndon was feeling quite lonely and ready to think about marriage. His high school and college romances had been with rather shy daughters of wealthy men – and the pattern repeated itself. That summer, while visiting his father in the office of the Texas Railroad Commission, Sam introduced him to a pretty young secretary, Eugenia Boehringer. Lyndon asked her for a date, but she turned him down.

In September, Lyndon called Eugenia again and asked her to arrange a blind date, which she did. When he came to the office to meet his date, a friend of Eugenia's was there. Her name was Claudia Alta Taylor. Eugenia had already told Lyndon all about Claudia, and he asked her to join him for breakfast at the hotel coffee shop the next day.

The next morning, Lyndon not only offered Claudia breakfast, but also a ride in his car. He soon learned that she was called "Lady Bird," a name bestowed on her by a family maid, who had said, "She's purty as a lady bird."

Lady Bird described that first outing: "He was tall and gangling and he talked incessantly. At first, I thought he was quite a repulsive young man. Then I realized he was handsome and charming and extremely bright. It would be hard to say what I thought."

On the drive, Lyndon told Lady Bird about his ambitions, his job, even how much insurance he carried – intensely personal things – and before the end of the day, he asked her to marry him. Lady Bird treated the proposal as a joke. For a young woman who was a loner, who saw herself as dowdy, shy, and a wallflower, it was hard to believe that Lyndon was serious.

Despite her shyness, Lady Bird had begun to show signs that she was ambitious and determined. She graduated from the University of Texas with honors, a Bachelor of Arts degree, and a teacher's certificate. Then she returned to the university for an additional year so she could get a second degree in her special interest—journalism. She also learned typing and shorthand because she felt "if you were really bright and knew and could use good English and got to be a secretary, you could probably advance to most any place in the business from running the business to marrying the boss." (She would later marry the boss and run her own business as well.)

In Pursuit of a Bride

It was early September of 1934 and Lyndon had only a few days before he had to return to Washington for the fall session. As always, he made the most of his time. The day after he proposed, he took Lady Bird to meet his parents. With smiles of approval from his parents, Lyndon now tried to impress Lady Bird by taking her to Richard Kleberg's King Ranch.

For two years, Lyndon had been sending notes to Kleberg's mother. He had met her on several occasions and had won her over. So it was no surprise when "Grandma" Kleberg declared to Lady Bird, "He's a fine young man. You should marry him."

It was not Mrs. Kleberg's approval Lady Bird sought; it was her father's. A week after they met, she invited Lyndon to stop at her home in Karnack, Texas, on his way back to Washington. It did not take long for her father to size up the young man. Taking Lady Bird aside after dinner, he commented, "Well, honey, you've brought home a lot of boys, but this time, I think you've brought home a man."

Though Lyndon repeated his marriage proposal before he left for Washington, Lady Bird held off giving a definite answer. For two months, letters flew back and forth between the young couple. In early November, Lyndon returned to Texas to see her. She agreed to an engagement but said she would never make such an important decision without her Aunt Effie's approval. Aunt Effie, who had raised Lady Bird since she was five years old, when her mother died, urged her to wait until she knew Lyndon better. But Lady Bird remembered her father's words, "If you wait until Aunt Effie is ready, you will never marry anyone. Besides, some of the best deals I ever made were made in a hurry."

And Lyndon was in a hurry. By the time they drove from Karnack to San Antonio to purchase an engagement ring, Lyndon had persuaded Lady Bird to get married immediately. He telephoned a friend in San Antonio to get the minister, the license, and St. Marks Episcopal Church, all by 6:30 P.M. At the last minute, the friend had to dash out to Sears, Roebuck to get a tray of wedding rings so Lady Bird could select one. She chose a ring costing $2.50.

The wedding date was November 17, 1934. No member of the bride or groom's family was present.

Chapter 4

Good Things Come in Threes

If Lady Bird Johnson was disappointed that Lyndon did not find time to do the things he had promised, she never let the outside world know. He did not discuss books, attend movies or theater, or even escort her on a tour of Washington, as he had said he would. Moreover, Lyndon was just as critical and demanding of his wife as he was of people who worked for him. He expected her to pay the bills, entertain guests at a moment's notice, lay out his clothes, and shine his shoes. He criticized her choice of clothes and often insisted on picking them out himself.

Housekeeping and cooking were new skills that Lady Bird had to learn, for she had been brought up in a household where servants did the domestic chores. Yet she mastered these as well as meeting Lyndon's other expectations. Despite all this, "Bird," as Lyndon always called her, showed a pleasant and calm face to all. It did not take long for friends to begin to see how bright she was and to sense her self-discipline.

THE NEW JOHNSON HOME

As a congressional secretary living in the basement of the Dodge Hotel, Lyndon had not been able to invite guests home. Now, with an apartment and Lady Bird to act as hostess, he could begin to socialize informally. The small apartment they shared on Kalorama Road became a haven where guests, expected and unexpected, were welcomed warmly by a gracious hostess. One frequent visitor was Sam Rayburn, a bachelor congressman from Texas who would later become one of the most beloved Speakers of the House.

An Important Friend

For a long time, Lyndon had been cultivating Sam Rayburn's friendship, but it was Lady Bird's genuine affection and sincere concern for Rayburn that made him adopt the newlyweds as the children he never had. The relationship would endure through arguments and disagreements — and would be a profitable one for the ambitious, young, congressional secretary.

In 1906, at the age of 24, Sam Rayburn ran successfully for the Texas legislature, where he became friends with Lyndon's father. The two Sams had much in common. They fought the interests of the railroad and banking money, and they refused the free railroad passes, free meals, and free hotel rooms that were offered to them by lobbyists.

Rayburn's dream was to become Speaker of the Texas House of Representatives, a congressman in Washington, and eventually, Speaker of the U.S. House of Representatives. By age 30, he had achieved his first two goals. Men in Washington soon learned what Sam's colleagues in Texas already knew, that the short, pudgy, feisty, bald-headed Rayburn was a man of integrity. Lobbyists could not buy him anything, not even a meal, nor would he take money for speeches or even traveling expenses. Rayburn's response to such suggestions was, "I'm not for sale."

Though elected to Congress in 1912 and re-elected continually, he would have to wait through 12 years of Republican control of the House and the seniority system to reach his goal. But when he did, he would serve as Speaker longer than any other in American history and bring a new power and dignity to the office. By the time Lyndon Johnson arrived in Washington, Sam Rayburn was a power to be reckoned with.

JOBS FOR YOUTH

By 1935, Lyndon was becoming desperate. His job seemed to be leading nowhere. Elected office seemed unlikely because he had no constituency in Texas. Then Lyndon was offered a well-paying job as a lobbyist. He was just about to accept when, in June 1935, President Roosevelt created the National Youth Administration (NYA). Because of the Great Depression, many young people had been forced to drop out of school because they lacked funds for books, bus fare, even shoes. Nor could they find jobs. The NYA was designed to find work for what people were beginning to call "The Lost Generation."

Roosevelt signed the Executive Order creating the NYA on a Tuesday morning. By that afternoon, Lyndon had already called Rayburn, Maury Maverick, Texas Senator Tom Connally, and Alvin Wirtz, a prominent Texas attorney and lobbyist who had been a state senator and for whom Lyndon had done a number of favors. Lyndon wanted the job of NYA director for the state of Texas, and he was calling to have his favors returned.

When Senator Connally approached Roosevelt, the President scoffed at the idea of giving the position to a 26-year-old without any administrative experience. It was Rayburn's visit that finally persuaded Roosevelt to appoint Lyndon Johnson to the post. It turned out to be a superb choice.

Lyndon Johnson, Administrator

When Lyndon called and asked, "Bird, how would you like to go to Austin?" she replied, "That's like asking, 'How would you like to go to Heaven?' Of course, we're going!"

It turned out to be one of the happiest times of their lives.

Finding a staff was easy. Lyndon had given many people patronage jobs—political appointments to regular party members. Now he began to call them in as members of his staff, people like Luther Jones as well as Willard Deason and others from his White Star days. One new addition was Herbert Henderson, a journalist, who took charge of public relations and would become Johnson's only speech writer during most of his time in Congress.

Finding suitable work projects for a state as huge and as diversified in climate and culture as Texas was much harder. The choice of projects had been left to state directors. The projects could not displace adult workers, nor could they be ones already funded by state or local government. Most importantly, the money had to be spent soon.

One of the first and most successful projects was a new concept, "roadside parks," which were areas beside newly constructed highways that offered shade trees, barbecue pits, and picnic benches. The project received excellent publicity. Lyndon traveled all over the state, meeting with mayors, and his picture appeared often in local newspapers. Invariably, the newspapers noted that he was the youngest state director of NYA in the country. Within a year, 135 parks were under construction and 3,600 young people were earning $30 a month. Other projects soon followed, such as improvement of school playgrounds, gravel paths along highways so children could walk safely to school, and even small "turnouts" so rural postmen would not create traffic hazards when they had to stop at farmers' mailboxes.

Helping the Underprivileged

This was only half the job. The other half was to find jobs for those young men and women who wanted to stay in school. This proved to be harder, for colleges and high schools had to fill out many forms and go through much red tape as student applications piled up in offices. Once again, Lyndon made his staff work six and seven days a week. Once again, as he had done in Kleberg's office, he used competition and criticism to spur on his employees. Lyndon was an astute reader of men, and he knew just when to use sarcasm (a type of bitter humor) and when to give a compliment. If a desk was cluttered with paper, Lyndon might growl, "I hope your mind's not as messy as that desk." And if the desk was finally cleared, he might grumble, "I hope your mind's not as empty as that desk."

Yet, despite the comments and hard work, most of the men stayed on the job. Those who could not stand the pace either quit or were eliminated. Loyalty was Lyndon's primary requirement for anyone who worked for him. Many worked not out of financial need but to attach themselves to what they saw was a rising star. Men like Deason remembered, "I knew that he would be moving into something with a bigger challenge. I had a sense of destiny with him."

The only portion of the NYA program for which Lyndon did not seek publicity was on the funds he appropriated for the employment of blacks and Mexican-American young-sters and for black colleges. Though he did not employ blacks on his staff, he was sincere about his feelings that the pro-gram was for poor people, which included many blacks and Mexican-Americans.

The bursar, or business officer, of Sam Houston Col-lege, a school for blacks, remembered, "We couldn't have paid our faculty except for Mr. Johnson. He'd send us our quota of money. Then off the record, he'd say, 'I've got a little extra change here. Can you find a place for it?' We could always find a place." Lyndon's efforts left a legacy of good will among the black Texas residents.

It was Eleanor Roosevelt, the First Lady, who had first urged her husband to create the NYA program, so it was only natural for her to visit Texas several times to see what was going on. On those occasions, Lyndon made sure to escort her around the state. It is not surprising, therefore, that her reports to the President included glowing comments on how much she was impressed with the young Texan.

TIME FOR AN ELECTION!

The banner headline for the February 23, 1937, *Houston Post* read "CONGRESSMAN JAMES P. BUCHANAN DIES." Lyndon had been touring with the state NYA director from Kansas when he saw the paper lying on a park bench. This was the chance he had been waiting for! The 10th Congres-sional District! That included his home in Austin and his boy-hood home in Johnson City.

It was true Lyndon was not as well known in the 10th District as he was in Kleberg's 14th, but he could make him-self better known. Lyndon could hardly wait for his Kansas visitor to leave. He immediately rushed back to Austin, where he had to speak to Lady Bird and contact Alvin Wirtz.

Wirtz, like Rayburn, had become another of Lyndon's mentors—a trusted teacher. He, too, had no son. He, too, was impressed with the dynamic young politician. If anyone could assess Lyndon's chances for the congressional seat, Al Wirtz could—and he did. Wirtz not only saw a rising star, he also saw a man who already knew his way around Washington and would be aggressive enough to help Wirtz in his role as a lobbyist for construction contractors and other interests he had.

Both Wirtz and Lady Bird gave Lyndon the green light, and his wife gave him his first financial backing. Wirtz had said Lyndon would need $10,000 to get his campaign going. Dependable as ever, Lady Bird quickly and quietly went to the phone.

"Daddy, would you please send me $10,000 of the inheritance Mother left me?"

At first, her father hesitated. Couldn't they get by on $5,000? But his daughter held firm, and when the bank opened on Monday morning, the funds needed to start Lyndon's first campaign were already deposited. Wirtz would later raise far more money, but it was Lady Bird's personal backing that gave Lyndon his start.

Wirtz also suggested the issue on which Lyndon would run. The 10th District was solidly behind President Roosevelt and his New Deal program. Johnson had to be more than just behind Roosevelt; he had to be "Roosevelt's Man." Whether he liked it or not, that meant Lyndon had to support Roosevelt's scheme to increase the number of Supreme Court justices from nine to 15. Johnson believed in the practical-minded Roosevelt and admired his ability to get things done. He wanted to be "Roosevelt's Man."

A political campaign needs three things – money, an issue, and an organization. For many candidates, the third item is a serious problem, but not for Lyndon. He had been preparing for this day for years. His first followers included Bill Deason, who borrowed $500 from the bank to put into the campaign and who offered his brand new car as a campaign car for Lyndon. Gene Latimer arranged for a leave of absence from his job with the Federal Housing Administration. Luther Jones and Herbert Henderson also joined the bandwagon.

Some Fatherly Advice

It was Lyndon's father who gave him the best advice. It looked as if there might be as many as 10 candidates filing for the special election, which was to be held in April. One of those mentioned was Buchanan's widow, who might be a sentimental favorite. Lyndon told Sam that he would wait until Monday to see if the widow was really going to run.

Sam exploded. "Doggone it, Lyndon! You never learn anything about politics! She's an old woman – too old for a fight. If she knows she's going to have a fight, she won't run. Announce now – and she won't run."

That Sunday afternoon, Lyndon announced his candidacy from the porch of his father's home. His father spoke on his son's behalf. Later Lyndon would describe how he "saw tears in his [father's] eyes as he told the crowd how terribly proud he was of me and how much hope he had for his country if only his son could be up there in the nation's capital with Roosevelt and Rayburn and all those good Democrats." It was a proud moment for the Johnson family.

On Monday, Mrs. Buchanan announced that she had decided *not* to enter the race.

Off and Running

If youth, enthusiasm, and tireless energy are needed to win an election, Lyndon had all three. While his men plastered the countryside and the towns with posters featuring Lyndon's smiling face and made sure that local newspapers carried items about him, Lyndon was meeting the public, 18 hours a day. He met with small groups of folks at courthouse squares and country stores. He spoke at well-attended barbecues, where the free beef and flowing beer mellowed the audience. And he rarely passed a barn without stopping, getting out of the car, and chatting with the farmer over his fence. He met every potential voter he could find, even if it meant driving 20 miles out of his way, down dirt roads, to find a voter too remote for radio or newspaper delivery.

Two days before the close of the campaign, Lyndon was speaking before a crowd of 400 people when he suddenly doubled up in pain. He stayed at the rally long enough to shake hands with folks from the audience and then he was rushed to the hospital—just in time. A few minutes more and he would have had a ruptured appendix. He received the election results in his hospital bed. He had won with 3,000 more votes than his nearest competitor.

LYNDON MEETS THE PRESIDENT

Congressman Lyndon Baines Johnson was on his way back to Washington, but this time he was going in style. With his connection with reporters in the nation's capital, even the *Washington Post* had a headline about him: "TEXAS SUPPORTER OF COURT CHANGE APPEARS ELECTED." Lyndon not only wanted to make sure that the President knew about his pro-Roosevelt campaign, he also wanted to be photographed with F.D.R.

*The Galveston handshake. The new congressman, Lyndon
Johnson (right), meets President Franklin D. Roosevelt for the
first time in Galveston, Texas. Between them is Texas Governor
James Allred (whose face would later be air-brushed out).*
(Lyndon Baines Johnson Library.)

Roosevelt was on a fishing trip off the coast of Texas,
so Lyndon asked the governor, James Allred, to arrange a
meeting. When the President's yacht sailed into Galveston Bay,
waiting on the dock was Governor Allred—and Lyndon Johnson. Not only did Lyndon have his picture taken with
Roosevelt, not only did the newspapers pick it up, but it became an important prop in his 1941 campaign for the U.S.
Senate. (By that time, the governor's face had been air-brushed
out of the picture.)

Roosevelt invited Lyndon to accompany him on the first
leg of his railroad journey back to Washington. By the time
the day was over, Lyndon was assured of a seat on the powerful

The new congressman and Lady Bird bid farewell to his parents as he departs by train for Washington in 1937. (Lyndon Baines Johnson Library.)

Naval Affairs Committee, and he had the telephone number of Thomas G. Corcoran, one of the President's key men.

Corcoran himself was a master of flattery, and he recognized Lyndon's talents for what they were. "Lyndon had one of the most incredible capacities for dealing with older men . . . I saw him talk to an older man and the minute he changed subjects, Lyndon was there ahead of him, saying what he wanted to hear—before he knew he wanted to hear it."

With an assist from Roosevelt and Corcoran, Lyndon became part of a group of bright young New Dealers. The group included James H. Rowe, a Harvard Law School alumnus, William O. Douglas, a former Yale Law School professor who would later serve as a justice on the Supreme Court, and his assistant, Abe Fortas, described as "the most brilliant legal mind to ever come out of Yale Law School." While other new congressmen were struggling to stay afloat, Lyndon Johnson was already swimming with the "big fish."

Chapter 5

The Whiz Kid of Congress

Even the inner circle of New Dealers could not help but be impressed by Lyndon's energy, his store of knowledge, and his ability to absorb information. If Lyndon gave his all for Kleberg's 14th District before, he outdid himself working for his own 10th District. One of his first efforts was to help Alvin Wirtz, his campaign manager, with the Marshall Ford Dam project.

REPAYING FAVORS

There had been several projects on the lower Colorado River, dams supposedly designed for flood control but whose primary purpose was more often the production of hydroelectric (water) power. By the time Lyndon entered the scene, one of these projects, the Marshall Ford Dam, was in serious trouble. In the rush to organize and to provide employment under the New Deal acts, errors had been made. The Bureau of Reclamation had spent millions of dollars on the project without the approval of the House Appropriations Committee, of which the deceased Representative Buchanan had been a powerful member. The new congressman, Lyndon Johnson, was not on the committee and had no seniority.

The building contractor for the dam, Herman Brown, badly needed money to complete the project. Brown's lawyer was Alvin Wirtz, and Wirtz knew just whom to contact— the congressman he had helped to elect, Lyndon Johnson. Though Lyndon could not call on the White House himself, he could make contact with Roosevelt through his new friend, Tommy Corcoran. When Corcoran spoke to Roosevelt about the project, the President's response was, "Give the kid the dam."

Roosevelt's support meant that enough loyal Roosevelt congressmen would vote for the dam through appropriate channels. The project received the financing and the authorization it needed.

Helping the Hill Country

As a congressman, Lyndon did more than respond to his constituents' requests and to lobbyists for Texas business interests. He also found every possible way of bringing money and assistance to the district he represented. When the United States Housing Authority was signed into law, he made sure that Austin received funds for slum clearance projects, providing a housing project for whites, one for blacks, and one for Mexican-Americans.

The undertaking dearest to his heart, however, was bringing electricity to the Hill Country. In 1937, electricity was an accepted part of life in most parts of the country; it was not so in Congressman Johnson's home territory. The Texas Power and Light Company could not afford to bring electric power lines to farmers who lived so far apart. The only source of power in small towns was a small 30 horsepower diesel engine. That supplied enough voltage for 10-watt bulbs—

certainly not enough for an electric appliance like a refrigerator or even a steam iron. There was no electricity for milking machines or water pumps, no hot water for washing dishes or clothes, no light for reading—and no radio.

In May 1936, Sam Rayburn shepherded the Rural Electrification Administration (REA) through Congress. Through the REA, funds were loaned to electric companies or to farmers to start electric companies. Non-profit organizations, like farmer cooperatives, would be given preference.

But the Hill Country folks were leery about the idea of forming a cooperative. The government regulations insisted that there had to be a minimum of three farms per mile before an application would be considered, and an REA agent had told them, "You have too much land and not enough people." The farmers were also afraid that electricity would be too costly for their limited incomes.

But Congressman Johnson was not one to give up so easily. He toured his district, brought the farmers together in meetings, and urged them to cooperate. He promised that he would do his part to see that the federal government made the proper allowances for the 10th District. And he kept his promise. Two years later, a federal loan of almost two million dollars was granted to the Pedernales Electric Cooperative. Electricity had finally come to the Hill Country.

The Brown Connection

When war erupted in Europe in 1939, Lyndon's role on the House Naval Affairs Committee increased. He disliked making speeches and getting involved in public debate, so he seldom spoke on the House floor to introduce or support bills. But as a member of the Naval Affairs Committee, he was able to help Herman Brown and his brother win a huge contract for the construction of the Corpus Christi Naval Air Station.

Though the Browns were generous in helping Lyndon to buy new automobiles at or below cost and inviting the Johnsons to their homes, Lyndon always carefully refused outright gifts. But the brothers had their first opportunity to really help Lyndon during the 1940 election year.

Johnson had no opposition for his own seat in the House, but he wanted to play a role in the national campaign. To keep his Texas connection happy, Roosevelt appointed Lyndon to assist the Democratic Congressional Campaign Committee. Unfortunately, the committee had very little money and could not help Democratic candidates in trouble. The Brown brothers were more than happy to help Lyndon by donating funds to the campaign committee, as did other friends of Lyndon's.

Within a week, there was over $45,000 in the campaign chest. In several key contests, the money that Lyndon personally allotted meant the difference between victory or defeat. As always, the candidates knew *who* had helped them, and so did President Roosevelt. After the election, he called Lyndon and thanked him for helping him maintain a Democratic-controlled Congress.

A RUN FOR THE SENATE

In April 1941, when one of the Texas senators, Morris Sheppard, died unexpectedly, Lyndon Johnson needed no consultations with friends or urging to run for the vacant Senate seat. Since this was a special election, he would not have to give up his seat in the House in order to run. Even if he lost, he would still retain his House seat, so he had nothing to lose.

Although Lyndon had a statewide network of friends from his two years in the National Youth Administration, he still was not very well known in most of Texas. He needed Roosevelt's support, and the President obliged by asking Lyndon to visit him in the White House just before a press conference. Lyndon made sure to greet the reporters as he left the Oval Office and to announce his candidacy "under the banner of Roosevelt."

Though more than 20 candidates announced they were running for the senatorial opening, only one eventually proved to be a powerful opponent. That was the governor of Texas, W. Lee "Pappy" O'Daniel, a businessman and radio personality who played country music and promised to "throw the professional politicians" out of Austin. That theme struck the right chord for many Texans, who could not understand why Texas, which produced more gas and oil than any other state and more sulfur than all the rest of the world put together, had little money for education and social services and a deficit of 19 million dollars.

At one point, when the polls showed the governor with 33 percent of the vote against 9 percent for Lyndon, Lyndon ended up in the hospital. Whatever the illness (his followers called it pneumonia), he came out two weeks later, thinner, more humble, and ready to fight!

It turned out to be one of the zaniest campaigns in history. Johnson was determined to fight O'Daniel on his own terms. He made fewer speeches and staged more entertainment. Lyndon's rallies included a six-man band, dancing girls, a harmonica player, and a female singer. If his opponent, Pappy, campaigned in his shirt sleeves, so did Lyndon. To top it all off, Lyndon's rallies offered a lottery, with U.S. Defense Bonds and Stamps handed out to those lucky enough to have their numbers called.

A Ballot Box Caper

By the end of election day, all the votes from the major cities were in, and Lyndon, announcing the results, began to celebrate. But all the votes were *not* in from rural Texas, and O'Daniel's supporters knew just how many more votes they needed to defeat Johnson. Two days later, the final votes were reported. Though some counties had telephoned results earlier, they had not been officially certified votes. When the final tally came in, many of the figures had changed. The election had been stolen from him! Lyndon did not risk a recount, for he feared it might reveal irregularities on the part of some of his own zealous supporters.

Despite the defeat, Roosevelt's support and warm feelings for Lyndon remained. The President called him for a chat and jokingly said to him, "Lyndon, apparently you Texans haven't learned one of the first things we learned up in New York State, and that is that when the election is over, you have to sit on the ballot boxes."

LIEUTENANT COMMANDER JOHNSON

For some time, relations had been cool between Sam Rayburn and Lyndon. The issue centered around John Nance Garner, a Texan who served twice as Vice-President under Roosevelt. When Garner broke with Roosevelt and decided to oppose him for the presidential nomination in 1940, Johnson was caught in the middle. As a loyal Texan, he needed Garner and the power he wielded in the state. But because Lyndon was a Roosevelt man, he hedged in giving any all-out support to Garner.

Rayburn did not approve of Garner's political stands, but

Garner had been very helpful in getting Sam the position of House majority leader. As Rayburn said, "Jack Garner is my friend." When Lyndon refused to commit himself to help Garner, relations between Rayburn and Johnson became very strained.

All of that changed, however, when Rayburn learned that Johnson had entered the U.S. Navy.

Reconciliation and a Silver Star

"If the day ever comes when my vote must be cast to send your boy to the trenches, that day . . . Lyndon Johnson [will] leave his Senate seat and go with him." While campaigning against Pappy O'Daniel, that was one of the promises Lyndon had made to the voters, and he soon realized his political reputation depended on his keeping his word.

When war broke out on December 7, 1941, Lyndon delivered on his promise. But how he kept it was a different matter. Because of his seat on the Naval Affairs Committee, he did not have to go through the tough naval training of the average officer. Instead, he received an instant commission as a lieutenant commander in the Navy. His first assignment was an office job in San Francisco.

For Sam Rayburn, there was no doubt about Lyndon's patriotism. Lyndon, too, seemed eager to revive the relationship. When Lyndon applied for and received an assignment in the South Pacific, Sam was at the jam-packed railroad station to bid farewell to Commander Johnson and to take a teary Lady Bird out for dinner.

Lyndon was sent overseas as part of a three-man team to evaluate the effectiveness of the military effort in the South Pacific. As a congressman, he was given VIP (very important person) treatment. He met General Douglas MacArthur in Australia and flew on a mission to bomb a Japanese base in New Guinea. The American bombers were attacked by two dozen Japanese fighters. (Some say the number of Japanese planes increased every time Johnson retold the story.) Bullets hit Lyndon's plane, but the pilot managed to return the plane safely to the American base. The crew noted Johnson's calm manner under fire.

Johnson saw no further action, but General MacArthur personally awarded him the nation's third highest honor, the Silver Star, for "coolness in spite of the hazard involved." On July 1, 1942, Roosevelt ordered all congressmen in military service back to Washington, unless they wished to resign their seats. (Four of them actually did.) Johnson chose to return to Washington.

A NEW JOHNSON FAMILY

In Lyndon's absence, Lady Bird and Sam Rayburn regained their former closeness. She also gained new confidence, for Lyndon had left her in charge of his congressional office. She turned out to be a very capable and efficient manager, and Lyndon began to view her with a new appreciation for her talents. Then, after 10 years of marriage and several miscarriages, on March 9, 1944, their first child, Lynda Bird, was born.

It was sometimes hard to know who enjoyed the baby's arrival more—her father or Sam Rayburn. When sister Luci arrived three years later, there were two little girls to be doted on. It was an especially happy time for Lyndon and his family, and Sam once more shared their closeness. He was not only a dear friend but much like a grandfather to Lynda and Luci, bouncing the girls on his knees and laughing as they chatted away.

Station KTBC

The arrival of the children, Lyndon's re-election to the House, and the reconciliation with Sam Rayburn were only part of the reasons for the family's happiness. When Lady Bird's father died, she inherited a large sum of money. On the advice of wealthy friends in Austin, she used a portion of her inheritance in 1943 to purchase a nearly bankrupt radio station, KTBC. Johnson critics and political opponents would later question whether the purchase was legal and proper for the wife of a congressman.

Johnson's position in the House may have smoothed the way for the Federal Communications Commission's approval of Lady Bird's ownership of the station, but there was nothing illegal in the transaction. Lady Bird proved to be a very competent manager. She had enough money to rebuild the station, which was returning a handsome profit by its second year of operation. With the money from this and other investments, the Johnsons were finally becoming financially secure. Lyndon Johnson was now a man of substance.

THE SENATE – NOW OR NEVER

In 1948, L.B.J., as he was frequently called, was faced with a crucial decision. Pappy O'Daniel had had enough of the Senate after one term, and his seat would be up for election. If Lyndon ran for the Senate this time, he would have to give up his House seat first, since it was not a special election. He would also be opposing a very popular governor, Coke Stevenson, and several other candidates, which meant there would have to be a run-off election after the Democratic primary. In the Texas of 1948, winning the Democratic nomination was equivalent to winning the election. Lyndon decided to run, and when the primary was held, Johnson came in second to Stevenson.

The run-off campaign came down to two issues, which candidate hated the communists more and which one hated labor unions more (very unpopular with big business in Texas). During the campaign, Johnson pictured himself as a World War II veteran and Stevenson (who was 60) as a man who had sat out the war, and who now was too old for the Senate. Johnson also portrayed himself as a poor boy, though he hopped from county to county in his private helicopter.

Once again, L.B.J. took sick three weeks before the run-off, and once again there were irregularities in the election returns, on *both* sides. Stevenson tried to keep Johnson's name off the election ballot. The case went to the Supreme Court, which refused to support an injunction (a restraining court order) against Johnson on the grounds that the highest court would then be deciding an election outcome. Eventually, Lyndon won the run-off and the election, but it was a narrow victory, certainly not an overwhelming vote of confidence. In the long run, *how* he achieved his seat turned out to be unimportant compared to *what* he achieved in the Senate once he got there.

Chapter 6
The Power and the Glory

W hat Lyndon Johnson wanted most when he returned to Washington was power in the Senate and to be re-elected. He had to prove to his electorate that he could be the best U.S. senator Texas ever had. He also needed to gain a national reputation so that he would be ready for his next goal, the vice-presidency or the presidency.

To accomplish this, Johnson had to do what he always did in new situations — learn everything about the system and discover who had the power. One person who helped him was a young, brash 20-year-old named Bobby Baker, who, as chief page in the Senate, was an expert on the business of the Senate. When L.B.J. first met Baker, he came right to the point, "I want to know who's the power over there, how you get things done, the best committees, the works." Baker was happy to oblige and soon became the key to Johnson's intelligence network.

Johnson also had to find an older man with power, one who would provide a father-son relationship such as he had enjoyed with Roosevelt and Rayburn. The new man Johnson courted was Senator Richard Russell from Georgia, the most powerful Democrat in the Senate and the chairman of the

Armed Services Committee. Russell, like Rayburn, was a lonely bachelor and loved being invited to the Johnson home for dinner or Sunday brunch. It did not take long for Lyndon to be appointed a member of Russell's important committee.

SETTING THE STAGE TO LEAD

The new Senate of 1948 included some men who would soon be well known on the national scene, especially Hubert Humphrey of Minnesota and Estes Kefauver of Tennessee. For the first two years, Johnson worked quietly behind the scenes. He sponsored no major legislation during that time. His priority had changed. Where before his energies had been directed to helping his constituency, now his efforts were channeled to making friends with his colleagues, getting to know how they operated, and helping to push various bills through the Senate. What Lyndon wanted to do was begin to shape national policy.

When the Senate majority leader, Democrat Scott Douglas of Illinois, lost his re-election bid to Republican Everett Dirksen in 1950, there was room at the top. Johnson was not ready to be majority leader, but he wanted the job of Democratic whip. The whip is responsible for directing party members, ensuring that the party's senators are in attendance when a voting call goes out. It requires long hours and hard work, but that was Johnson's strength. With the help of Russell and 12 Democratic senators, former members of the House who had been contacted by Sam Rayburn, Lyndon won the position.

The job did not offer any power, but it did take Lyndon out of the rut of being just another freshman senator. And when the majority leader was out campaigning or making a speech, Lyndon took over, and he made sure to make the most of every opportunity.

Sectional Differences

Lyndon hated labels. When he fought an issue in support of Texas oil interests, he was called a conservative. If he tried to support public housing, he was tagged as a liberal. Johnson believed that politics was the art of compromise, that it was better to get a needed bill passed, even if it was greatly changed from its original form. Some action, he reasoned, was better than none.

Part of the problem was that the country was divided by regional issues. What was good for the Northeast was often hated by the South, and vice versa. Lyndon looked for issues that bridged regions, that could be generally supported by the Democratic Party.

As Democratic whip, Johnson worked for two years under a rather ineffective majority leader, Ernest McFarland of Arizona. But Lyndon was willing to serve his apprenticeship, for it gave him a formal position and took him a step nearer towards his goal of becoming majority leader. His new constituency was the nation, and as always, he was determined to serve it well.

Minority Leader

In 1952 the Democrats lost control of the Senate by one vote during the landslide election of President Dwight D. Eisenhower. McFarland was one of the senators who went down in the defeat. It did not take long for Lyndon to line up the required votes, and in 1953 he became minority leader of the Democrats in the Senate.

In that role, Lyndon took control of the Democratic Policy Committee, which decided which bills the Democrats would push. He also directed the Steering Committee, which decided which committee assignments were given to deserving senators.

Being the minority leader was, surprisingly, a plus for Johnson. Now it was the Republicans who were responsible for getting their legislative ideas through Congress and the Democrats who constituted the loyal opposition. With only a one-vote margin, Eisenhower strategists needed Johnson's help to enact bills. He held the power to pick and choose which issues the Democrats would support, and he was cautious to choose only those issues which he knew he could rally his party behind.

MAJORITY LEADER

When the Republican majority in the Senate was overturned in the 1955 elections, Lyndon became majority leader. Such a rise to power had never happened to a freshman senator before. Within a year, he was already being talked about as a possible Democratic candidate for the presidency.

Now Lyndon was at his very best. He put in 15-hour days in the Senate cloakroom, offices, and halls to corral votes. He used all the information his aides could find to bring his fellow Democratic senators around to his way of thinking. He learned everything he could about each senator, for he needed to know (sometimes even before they knew themselves) just how each one would vote. It was hard to withstand Lyndon's intelligent arguments, and his colleagues had to concede that he was always well prepared with the facts. He was a master of "gentle arm-twisting" to gain the votes he needed.

On several occasions Lyndon kept the Senate working late into the night to get a bill passed. "What's the hurry?" complained one senator to another. "After all, Rome wasn't built in a day." The second senator sighed and answered, "True—but Lyndon Johnson wasn't the foreman on the job."

With an eye on his future, Lyndon found ways to win

converts to his side or have them feel indebted to him. He argued for increasing the number of seats on important committees so junior senators could serve on at least one important committee, and he took full credit when the idea was adopted.

Lyndon also influenced the Senate legislative process itself. He realized that most of the real action took place behind the scenes, not on the floor of the Senate. Because floor debates and speeches were time-consuming and rarely changed a legislator's mind, Lyndon worked hard to limit such discussions. He counted his success in the large number of bills that were passed while he was the majority leader.

FIGHTING McCARTHY

Of all of his many achievements as Democratic Party leader in the Senate, he was proudest of three. The first was his handling of the McCarthy issue while he was minority leader, the second was his record on civil rights, and the third was his support of the space program.

In 1953, when Johnson was minority leader, Senator Joseph McCarthy of Wisconsin was chairman of the Government Operating Committee and the Permanent Investigation Subcommittee. He had begun investigating Communists in government while seeking a campaign issue for his re-election. When the issue attracted large newspaper interest, McCarthy began a full-blown assault on searching out Communist sympathizers in the government, eventually attacking such high government officials as former President Harry Truman and former Secretary of State Dean Acheson. Few, if any, of the accusations were supported by facts.

When fellow senators approached Lyndon to do something about McCarthy's lies and the destruction of reputations caused by his actions, Lyndon held them off, explaining that the timing had to be right. One day, while discussing the problem with Senator Hubert Humphrey of Minnesota, Johnson said, "If you're going to kill a snake with a hoe, you have to get it with one blow at the head." In his usual way, Johnson would not undertake a task until he was reasonably sure of success. He also cautioned his fellow senators not to publicly oppose McCarthy, because McCarthy had enough public support that he would find ways to retaliate.

Lyndon Kills a Snake

In January 1954 McCarthy began a campaign against Communists and Communist sympathizers in the U.S. Army, and he included several generals on his list. The Senate decided that it would hold hearings on McCarthy's accusations about the Army. As plans for the hearings were being set up, Lyndon approached Senator John McClellan, one of the three Democratic members of McCarthy's subcommittee. Lyndon told McClellan that whatever concessions he had to make, he should insist that the hearings be televised. Johnson was convinced that McCarthy would not be able to survive exposure to television — that when millions of Americans saw McCarthy's taunting, public abuse of American citizens, they would turn against him.

The televised hearings went on for months, and just as Lyndon had predicted, the American public began to tire of McCarthy's groundless accusations and started to turn against him. Meanwhile, quietly and carefully, Johnson worked behind the scenes. He urged the establishment of a Select Committee consisting of six senators, three from each party, whose sole job would be to investigate McCarthy's actions. For six weeks, the Select Committee met privately gathering evidence. Following the November 1954 elections, the Senate finally debated the Select Committee's recommendations.

For the first time, Lyndon broke his silence and made one of his rare speeches on the Senate floor. "In my mind there is only one issue here – morality and conduct," he said. "Each of us must decide whether we approve or disapprove of certain actions as standard for senatorial integrity. I have made my decision."

On December 2, 1954, the Senate voted to condemn McCarthy. Every single Democrat present voted with Johnson and against McCarthy. Johnson's carefully thought-out plan had achieved the end of McCarthyism.

CIVIL RIGHTS AND THE SPACE PROGRAM

Looking back at his years in the Senate, Johnson would later cite the Civil Rights Act of 1957 as his single greatest legislative achievement and probably the most demanding test of his Senate leadership. Until 1957, Lyndon's record on civil rights was anything but positive. He personally believed in equal opportunities for blacks, as witnessed by his policies while a state director for the National Youth Administration. However, he recognized that most of Texas and the South were against increasing the rights and political power of blacks. He had consistently voted against civil rights legislation, fearful that any other action would mean defeat at the polls for him. Yet if he expected to be a power on the national scene, he knew he would have to move closer to the views of liberal northerners. He had to find a position that he could defend both to the North *and* the South.

The Eisenhower administration had originated the civil rights bill, and Republicans were only too happy to push for its passage, seeing it as a way to split the Democrats. The bill had several sections which caused regional conflicts. To southerners, Johnson argued that it was only reasonable for blacks to have voting rights. To appease northerners, Johnson fought for a constitutional amendment that would eliminate poll taxes, a fee paid for the privilege of voting. He warned southern Democrats that if they attempted to block a civil rights bill, it might tempt northerners to offer a more radical measure next time.

The compromise bill was far from the one President Eisenhower had hoped to achieve, but it did pass the Senate by a vote of 72–18 and was an opening wedge for tougher bills in the future. For Johnson, it was a great personal victory. He had maintained party unity, prevented further regional conflict, and won applause from the press and the public. Later, as President of the United States, he would have another opportunity to improve his stand on civil rights.

The Fight for a Space Program

Johnson's third major achievement dealt with space—a subject of interest and expertise that few members of Congress understood. During the Korean War (1950–1953), Johnson had directed much of his energies toward his work on the Armed Forces Committee and had become chairman of the Preparedness Subcommittee. Here he developed an interest in space exploration. At that time, the government and the public showed little awareness of its potential. All that changed on October 4, 1957, when Sputnik, a tiny Soviet satellite, was launched into space.

Suddenly, the American public was awakened. A torrent of self-criticism flooded every phase of American life. Especially harsh words were directed against the nation's educational system, which critics claimed failed to provide the kind of scientific and technological training that the Soviets had. There was now a rush to improve the teaching of science and mathematics in the nation's schools.

The Space Race

A cloudless night sky, perfect for viewing the stars—and somewhere overhead, the Russian satellite Sputnik was orbiting the earth. Lyndon Johnson remembered that night well, October 4, 1957, for he had heard the news on television while at his ranch. He went outdoors, lifted his eyes skyward, and realized that the world would never be the same again. The Space Age had begun, and the Soviet Union had a running start. But that night, Senator Johnson determined that the United States would catch up quickly, if he had anything to do about it.

As chairman of the Senate Subcommittee on Preparedness, Johnson launched a congressional investigation into America's space program. The inquiry received national publicity, for it brought in many eminent scholars who told of the possibility of making a round trip to the moon in the not-too-distant future. The ensuing fanfare raised America's awareness of the need for greater research and better training of students in mathematics and science. With the passage of the National Aeronautics and Space Act in 1958, the new National Aeronautics and Space Administration received more than four billion dollars for rocket and missile research.

When John F. Kennedy was elected President in 1960, he included space research as part of his New Frontier program. Was the idea of a man on the moon in 10 years really a possibility? As Kennedy's chairman for the

Space Council, Vice-President Lyndon Johnson pulled together the best minds on the subject he could find, and they concluded that the project *could* be done. Based on this research, Congress approved a space program designed to send an American to the moon before 1970.

On April 12, 1961, Soviet astronaut Yuri Gagarin became the first man to orbit the earth in a space ship. Not quite a year later, American astronaut John Glenn followed Gagarin's feat. For several years, both nations traded leads sending their astronauts farther and farther out into space for longer and longer periods of time. Then, in 1965 the American public was elated to watch their astronauts hook up with a second space vehicle and take a walk in space. However, the American program suffered a serious setback two years later when the nation was shocked and saddened by the death of three NASA astronauts in a fire in a space capsule during a training accident.

The race to the moon was eventually won by the United States, and within the timeline set by President Kennedy. On July 20, 1969, Edwin Aldrin planted the American flag on the surface of the moon. President Johnson lived to see the landing, though most of the credit for the success of the space program was given to his predecessor, President John Kennedy.

Lyndon was one of the few men in Congress with the knowledge, the interest, and the power to take action. In 1958 Johnson, who rarely authored any legislation, took the initiative in sponsoring the National Aeronautics and Space Act, which created the National Aeronautics and Space Administration (NASA). As a result of his efforts, one of NASA's largest facilities was built in Houston, Texas. Lyndon's interest did not cease with the passage of this act, but continued through his later years of public service.

TIME FOR A CHANGE

Too many Democrats! "Believe me, they'll be hard to handle." That was Sam Rayburn's warning when the elections of 1958 gave the Democrats a 2 to 1 majority in both the Senate and the House. No longer did Lyndon have to worry about having enough votes. His problem now was to keep those votes in line. For several years, the voters had been sending more and more liberal-minded men to Congress. Few of these senators had openly rebelled against Lyndon's leadership, but with the class of 1958, the majority leader was finding it increasingly difficult to control the votes of so many Democrats.

At one point, when Johnson pressed Senator Edmund Muskie of Maine on how he would be voting, the new senator smiled and replied softly, "Well, Senator, I think I'll follow your advice and just wait until they get to the M's"—a line Johnson had used himself on several occasions. Lyndon was not amused.

More and more, Lyndon was finding that the job of majority leader was not as satisfying as it had been. He began to think seriously of a career change. Perhaps he would give up politics altogether and devote his energies to his broadcasting station. Or perhaps he would run for the presidency. As customary with Johnson, politics won out. The next step was President of the United States.

Chapter 7
Marking Time

L yndon was furious! It could not be true! For a man who boasted of his good health, who could put in a 15-hour workday and then eat, drink, and talk until late into the night, the idea of having a heart attack was unthinkable. The warning signs of the illness had been there for months, including that morning in July 1955. He had lost his temper with reporters at a press conference. He had bolted down a conference lunch of frankfurters and beans while smoking several cigarettes. Hoping to have a relaxing weekend, he had been driven by his chauffeur to a friend's beautiful Virginia estate. On arrival, Lyndon insisted that the pains he was having in his chest were only a "bellyache." Nevertheless, a doctor was called and immediately rushed Lyndon by ambulance to Bethesda Naval Hospital, just outside of Washington.

Even as L.B.J. was being wheeled into the hospital elevator, he could not resist joking with a pale and shaken Lady Bird. Remembering that he had just ordered two suits from his tailor, he said, "Tell him to go ahead with the blue suit. We can use that no matter what happens."

Johnson was so critically ill that he remained in the hospital for five weeks. Despite his worries that his career might be over, the illness probably lengthened his life. Once he got home, he began a careful routine. He cheered visitors with the news that he had given up smoking, was watching his diet, and was taking naps every afternoon. Lady Bird helped by watching Lyndon constantly to make sure that the doctor's orders were being followed.

Most gratifying to Lyndon were the messages of affection that poured in from all over the country. President Eisenhower drove to Bethesda to visit him. Vice-President Richard Nixon spent an hour briefing him on foreign affairs. For a man who needed constant assurance that he was loved and admired, the telegrams, flowers, and letters reassured the ailing majority leader. By early autumn he was ready to travel to his ranch in Texas for the final recuperation period.

HOME ON THE RANCH

For Lyndon, owning a ranch in the Hill Country had long been a dream, and in 1951 the dream had come true. The ranch had belonged to an aunt and uncle, and was a place he had visited often during his boyhood. After purchasing the ranch, Lyndon applied the same zeal to the house along the Pedernales River as he did to politics. In time, it became a showplace, where politicians, reporters, heads of state, and friends were treated to the Johnson brand of Texas hospitality. An affair would usually begin with a hair-raising ride around the ranch with Lyndon at the wheel of his white limousine, pointing out the deer herd or the family graveyard. That would be followed by a real chuck wagon barbecue, with checkered tablecloths, coal oil lanterns, and all the servers attired in western clothes.

For Lyndon, the ranch was a place where he could revive his tired body or flagging spirits. It was where he recovered from his heart attack and previous illnesses, and where he returned to spend the years following his presidency.

1960: KENNEDY VERSUS JOHNSON

In 1956 both John F. Kennedy and Lyndon Johnson wanted to test their potential as presidential candidates by being nominated for the vice-presidency. Both, however, were later relieved that they had *not* been on the badly defeated Democratic ticket led that year by Adlai Stevenson.

Early in 1960, however, John Kennedy began campaigning again—this time for President. In one state Democratic primary after another, Kennedy won delegates. And where was Lyndon Baines Johnson? Although L.B.J. insisted that he was *not* a candidate for the presidency, friends and colleagues were urging him to announce his candidacy. One of those who tried hardest to get Lyndon to run was Sam Rayburn. Pounding his fists, Sam declared, "He has to run. He just owes it to his country!" But Johnson persisted in refusing, arguing that there was too much work to be done in the Senate and he "had to tend the store."

By the time Lyndon Johnson met the press on July 5 to announce his candidacy, it was too late. His indecision had killed his chances for getting the party nomination. What Johnson had failed to take into account was the changing national scene. Presidential candidates were no longer being elected by cigar-chomping politicians in smoke-filled caucus rooms at national conventions. Rather, candidates were being selected by well-organized state-by-state primary races, with delegates being committed to a candidate long before a convention.

Arriving in Los Angeles on July 8 for the opening of the Democratic National Convention, Johnson realized that he had neither the organization nor the time to stop the Kennedy bandwagon. In the new politics of 1960, the well-oiled Kennedy organization won the presidential nomination for its candidate on the first ballot.

Kennedy Makes an Offer

The call came at 8:35 A.M. It was John Kennedy. Could he come down to Johnson's suite at 9:30? By the time Kennedy arrived, Lyndon had made a series of phone calls to those congressmen closest to him. If Kennedy was going to ask him to accept the vice-presidency, he wanted to hear all the pros and cons. Johnson could not help but be flattered when Jack Kennedy personally asked him to take the office, but he asked Kennedy for time to think it over. He especially wanted to hear Lady Bird's and Rayburn's feelings.

At first, Sam vehemently opposed the idea. But after meeting later with Kennedy, he realized that without Lyndon, the race might go to the Republican nominee, Richard Nixon, a man whom Sam despised. Rayburn advised Lyndon to accept. When Lyndon teased him about changing his mind, Sam replied, "Well, I'm a darn sight smarter this morning than I was last night."

Lady Bird had her own personal reasons for urging Lyndon to accept. Ever since his heart attack, she had worried about her husband's health. It was true he watched his diet and no longer smoked, but he still persisted in working long and crazy hours. She could see the strain taking its toll. She too, pressed her husband to accept. Lady Bird knew that a Vice-President does not have as many stressful responsibilities as a President does.

Johnson and Kennedy both knew that to win they had to present a united Democratic Party. On the opening day of the campaign in Boston in September, Johnson coined the term "the Boston-Austin Axis" to describe the party's solidarity. With Lyndon's help in bringing along Texas and the South, the Kennedy-Johnson ticket won the election in a very tight race.

Presidential candidate John F. Kennedy (left) and vice-presidential candidate Lyndon B. Johnson meet the press on August 1, 1960, just before a special session of Congress. (Library of Congress.)

MR. VICE-PRESIDENT

In his lifetime, Lyndon Johnson had learned how to assume leadership and how to accept the role of respectful subordinate. He much preferred the role of "big daddy" to that of "dutiful son." But as Vice-President, he had to subordinate his ideas and wishes to those of the man he now served, John F. Kennedy. Though it must have been hard for a man of Johnson's energy and ambition to do so, he was a loyal and willing servant of the Kennedy administration.

Johnson had hoped that he could make more of the position than his predecessors had. Kennedy did include Johnson in meetings of the National Security Council in order to keep him informed on foreign policy and to seek his opinion. But the usually outspoken Johnson refused to give more than a mumbled response. He worried that any recommendations he made would be labeled as "Johnson proposals," and he was unwilling to have that on record should an idea prove unsuccessful. In looking ahead to the elections in 1968, he wanted to keep his record as clear as possible of any major mistakes.

Johnson might have been useful to President Kennedy as a liaison to Congress, but he was rarely asked to do so by the Kennedy staff. Lyndon had also been very hurt by a rebuff from his Senate colleagues.

Senator Mike Mansfield, who had taken over as majority leader, asked his colleagues to allow Johnson to continue to act as chairman of the Senate Democrats whenever they met in formal conferences. Clearly, this was a breach of the separation of powers, for the Vice-President was a member of the executive branch of government and the Senate was a part of the legislative branch. Even some of his closest friends in Congress voted down the idea. Johnson felt very much left out.

Stand-in for the President

Without power or influence in either the executive or legislative branch of government, Lyndon retreated to the tasks
that Kennedy assigned to him—and in these, he was determined to be outstanding. One of the tasks Kennedy assigned
was to serve as the President's emissary. As such, Lyndon
might lack power, but he did have status. He was sent to represent the President at funerals of heads of state, to celebrate
the country of Senegal's independence, and to make official
visits to the Republic of China, India, Pakistan, Vietnam, and
the Philippines. On these visits he loved the crowds who came
to see him. He could not resist getting out of his car, walk-
ing among the people and shaking hands as if he were running for office. He would often tell the people he met, "You-all
come to see me in Washington."

Before he became Vice-President, Lyndon had hardly
been out of the country. He spoke no foreign language and
had little understanding of the culture of countries other than
his own. But he had certain advantages: he had no prejudices,
and he had a natural sympathy with people. On the other hand,
some of his demands for personal amenities, such as a certain type of shower head or a special oversized bed, as well
as his constant changing of plans and lack of courtesy drove
embassy officials wild. Yet, he could be a real "charmer" when
the occasion demanded it.

The Berlin Wall

Lyndon's greatest moment abroad as Vice-President occurred
in August 1961. Communist East Germany had closed off all
travel routes between East and West Germany and was building a concrete wall between East and West Berlin. The only
way to get to democratic West Berlin was over East German
roads. Kennedy decided to send United States troops across

these roads to test the East German blockade. Johnson undertook the assignment of going to West Berlin to represent the American government, knowing that if the East German guards stopped the American troops or he failed to calm the fears of the West Germans, the situation could lead to World War III.

The reception Vice-President Johnson received when he arrived in West Berlin was spectacular. Almost a million West Germans were on hand to greet him. At a special session of the West German Parliament, he echoed the words of the Declaration of Independence in pledging "our lives, our fortunes, and our sacred honor" to the defense of West Berlin. On August 20, he was on hand to greet the first U.S. troops who had dared to reopen the road from West Germany to West Berlin. For Lyndon Johnson, it was one of his shining hours.

Assignments on the Domestic Front

Two areas that President Kennedy specifically assigned to his Vice-President were the space program and civil rights. Knowing of Johnson's efforts on behalf of the space program in the Senate, Kennedy appointed Lyndon chairman of the National Space Council. During his tenure, the amount of federal funds channelled into the program was increased, and the timetable for space exploration was speeded up. As a result, the United States was able to land a man on the moon within the 10 years Kennedy had said it would take to do so.

Johnson was also made chairman of the Committee on Equal Employment. This committee had the responsibility of eliminating racial discrimination in those businesses that had contracts with the federal government. It was a first step toward erasing all discrimination in employment. Johnson told the committee staff, "Let's make it *fashionable* to end discrimination."

Vice-President: To Be or Not to Be

Does it pay to take the position of Vice-President? Is it a road to the presidency? The men who wrote the Constitution created the office of Vice-President in order to provide a replacement for the President in case he died or became too ill to conduct the nation's affairs. The Vice-President has very little power, but he does have a great deal of status. In some respects, the role is similar to that of a crown prince, who handles many ceremonial tasks for the king and is in training to take over the reins when the king dies. In the case of the Vice-President, however, it is not always certain that he will finally attain the top job of President.

In fact, only four Vice-Presidents—John Adams, Thomas Jefferson, Martin Van Buren, and George Bush—served their full terms in that position and then were elected President. Of the Vice-Presidents who gained the presidency because of the death of the President, only four—Theodore Roosevelt, Calvin Coolidge, Harry Truman, and Lyndon Johnson—went on to win the next election on their own.

Four Presidents ascended to the presidency because of a fatal illness of their predecessors. When William Henry Harrison caught pneumonia during his inauguration and died 31 days later, John Tyler took over. Warren G. Harding died after a trip to Alaska, leaving Calvin Coolidge to carry on. Millard Fillmore and Harry Truman also became President when Presidents Zachary Taylor and

Franklin D. Roosevelt, respectively, suc-
cumbed to illness.

Lyndon Johnson, who succeeded John F.
Kennedy, was one of four Vice-Presidents
who gained the highest office in the land
when the President was assassinated. Another Johnson, Andrew Johnson, took over
when Abraham Lincoln was killed. When
President James A. Garfield was shot to
death by a mentally disturbed office-seeker,
Chester Arthur took over. Theodore Roosevelt
became President when William McKinley was
killed by an anarchist at the Pan-American Ex-
position in Buffalo, New York.

One Vice-President, Gerald Ford, completed the President's term of office due to a
resignation. Rather than submit to impeach-
ment proceedings because of possible mis-
conduct in office, President Richard Nixon
resigned.

Is the office of Vice-President a challeng-
ing one? Many American Vice-Presidents have
had some comment to make about their experiences in the office. The first Vice-
President, John Adams, called it ''the most
insignificant office that ever the invention of
man contrived or his imagination conceived.''

Shortly after becoming President, his
brother chided Lyndon Johnson about the
way he was pushing himself. ''This pace will
kill you,'' said his brother. To which Lyndon
replied, ''These first few weeks have been
kinda hectic, but things will settle down
pretty soon. Ain't near as bad as being Vice-

President. Not being able to do *anything* will wear you down sooner than hard work."

Thomas Marshall, who served as Woodrow Wilson's Vice-President for eight years, told this story to describe his feelings: "Once there were two brothers. One ran away to sea, the other was elected Vice-President, and nothing was ever heard of either of them again."

In his own salty manner, Texan John Nance Garner, who served for two terms as Vice-President under Franklin Roosevelt, may have summed it up best: "The job is not worth a pitcher full of warm spit."

For a man who had moved gingerly in attacking civil rights and who believed in conciliation (to make opposing sides agree by compromise) as the best weapon to end discrimination, Johnson did not seem to move fast enough to satisfy his critics. Robert Kennedy, as the attorney general, supervised all civil rights matters and faced constant demands from black leaders. He often prodded Lyndon to take a more aggressive stand on civil rights, and Johnson resented the younger Kennedy's pushiness. Yet, using a combination of threats and promises of favorable publicity for those firms who complied with the new federal measures, Lyndon did make considerable progress toward eliminating racial discrimination in employment.

ASSASSINATION!

There were times during those years as Vice-President when Lyndon thought seriously about quitting after Kennedy's first term rather than being on the ticket in 1964. Kennedy had personally always been more than courteous to Lyndon. Kennedy had included him in Cabinet meetings, the Johnsons were invited to all the major social events at the White House, and Kennedy had publicly stated that he wanted Lyndon to serve a second term with him.

On November 22, 1963, Johnson discovered that he could not retreat. His options were closed. On that day, the Kennedys and the Johnsons were in Dallas, looking ahead to the 1964 election, drumming up support for the administration in Texas and the South. That day ended in Kennedy's assassination and Johnson's rise to the presidency.

Sadly, it was not as Lyndon had imagined it. There was no formal inauguration, no cheering crowds, no television coverage—just a few brief and somber moments in the presidential plane. When the plane landed at Andrews Air Force Base near Washington at six that evening, it was already getting dark. As the new President walked down the steps of the plane, the lights of television cameras covered his every move. Waiting at the bottom was a solemn and stunned group of congressmen, Cabinet members, and people from the diplomatic corps.

After a few moments, Johnson walked over to the microphones that had been set up. In the eerie shadows of the camera lights, he read the few words he had prepared on the plane for his first public speech as President.

"This is a sad time for all people. We have suffered a loss that cannot be weighed. For me it is a deep personal tragedy. I know that the world shares the sorrow that Mrs. Kennedy and her family bear. I will do my best. That is all I can do. I ask for your help—and God's."

Chapter 8

The Great Society

L yndon B. Johnson now had the ultimate power – and the final responsibility. By the time the plane carrying him back to Washington from Dallas had rolled to a stop, Lyndon had already planned what the themes of his first weeks in office would be – continuity and unity.

The nation had been shaken by the horror of that day in Dallas, replayed over and over again on television. The trauma of the assassination had turned the public admiration of the youthful and charismatic President into adoration of a fallen idol. In many ways, it made Johnson's task much more difficult.

To reassure a shattered nation, Johnson had to keep the Kennedy team intact. He also knew that during the period of mourning and transition, he had to soften his words and his actions, and restrain his naturally expansive personality. The fact that so many of the Kennedy team remained is a compliment to Johnson's tactful manners during this period.

Johnson also knew that he had to bring the nation together. The country had been torn by riots in Birmingham, Alabama, in May of that year. He decided to invoke the slain President's name to gain passage of legislation that the late President had found stalled in Congress. Advisors warned him that it would never get through, but the new President retorted, "Well, what the hell's the presidency for?"

A Christmas-card portrait presented to close friends and employees in 1963. At the left are the daughters of the President and Mrs. Johnson, Lynda Bird and Luci Baines. (Lyndon Baines Johnson Library.)

Just before Thanksgiving Johnson decided to speak to a televised joint session of Congress. Although not an electrifying public speaker, his quiet, forceful manner and well-chosen words beamed to homes all over the nation set a tone for his presidency and the work ahead:

> No memorial oration or eulogy could more eloquently honor President Kennedy's memory than the earliest possible passage of the civil rights bill for which he fought so long. We have talked long enough in this country about equal rights. We have talked for one hundred years or more. It is time now to write the next chapter—and to write it in the books of law.

I profoundly hope that the tragedy and the torment of these terrible days will bind us together in new fellowship, making us one people in our hour of sorrow.

THE 1964 CIVIL RIGHTS BILL

As a congressman, Lyndon Johnson had been a latecomer in supporting civil rights legislation. As majority leader of the Senate, he had urged compromise and conciliation to get such legislation passed. But as President of the United States, he would not accept anything but passage of a total civil rights package. He told members of the Senate that he would out-wait any attempts to delay action, and he promised that he would hold round-the-clock sessions until the bill was passed in its entirety. Under such a threat, southern opposition collapsed.

To prove his dedication to the cause, on New Year's Eve, 1963, Johnson arrived at the segregated faculty club of the University of Texas escorting a black woman, Gerri Washington, one of his secretaries. Secret Service men hovered nearby. Not a word of protest was heard that evening. Two days later, a member of the faculty club called and asked to bring two black guests. He was told that there would be no problem since the "President of the United States integrated us on New Year's Eve."

The 1964 civil rights bill was one of the most important pieces of legislation ever passed by Congress. It was a broad bill, protecting citizens against discrimination and segregation in employment, voting, education, and in such public places as restaurants, hotels, movie houses, and stadiums. It was the wedge that opened the door to a flood of civil rights and welfare bills that would be passed in the next few years under the slogan "The Great Society."

President Johnson meeting with Martin Luther King, Jr. (left) and other civil rights leaders in 1964. (Lyndon Baines Johnson Library.)

President Johnson signs the Civil Rights Act of 1964 in the East Room of the White House. Mrs. Johnson is seated in the front row. In the second seat to her left is Robert Kennedy, attorney general during the administration of his brother, John F. Kennedy. (Lyndon Baines Johnson Library.)

THE GREAT SOCIETY

Lyndon had successfully carried through the transition from the Kennedy to the Johnson administrations, and in the early months of 1964 was proving his talents as a dynamic, activist President. He had appointed Esther Peterson as the first special assistant for consumer affairs, had declared a war on poverty, and had gotten a tax cut through the legislature. Congress had approved a constitutional amendment to abolish the poll tax, and the amendment was now on its way to the states for ratification.

The President now needed to think about the upcoming election. He needed a phrase, an expression that would be identified with his administration as "The New Deal" had worked for Franklin Roosevelt and "The New Frontier" had for John Kennedy. The final selection was "The Great Society," coined by Richard Goodwin, one of his speech writers.

As Johnson envisioned The Great Society, it would be a place with no poverty or racial injustice. Cities would be places where "the water we drink, the food we eat, the very air we breathe" would no longer be threatened by pollution. Schools would be places where every child would have all the education he or she could absorb, and there would be "full social security" for "every older man and woman." There was something for everyone in this vision. It was a phrase that led the public to great expectations. What Johnson had not anticipated was that it could also lead to disappointment and frustration.

ELECTION: 1964

Johnson had gained his Senate seat in a protested election and had become President as a result of an assassination. What he wanted now was a mandate from the people, a landslide election, to prove that the people really wanted and admired him.

Yet Johnson had the same wavering concerns that always nagged at him—he was not good enough for the job; there were problems that might have no easy solutions. The day after the 1964 Democratic National Convention opened in Atlantic City, New Jersey, he penned a statement that he would only serve out Kennedy's term. However, he never delivered it publicly because his press secretary and Lady Bird reassured him that he was the man for the job.

On the third day of the convention, Johnson flew to At-

Campaigning in North Carolina in 1964. President Johnson, who won a landslide re-election, thoroughly enjoyed meeting and shaking hands with the people. (Lyndon Baines Johnson Library.)

lantic City in time to view on television the nominating speech by Texas Governor John Connally. He heard the approving roar of the crowd, and he loved every glorious moment. Though not scheduled to appear that evening, he entered the convention center triumphantly to a cheering and applauding audience. He accepted the nomination and announced the selection of his running mate, Hubert Humphrey, his old friend from Senate days.

A Landslide at Last

Senator Barry Goldwater of Arizona was the Republican presidential candidate. During the Republican primaries, his opponents had painted Goldwater as a man who would do away with the Social Security system and risk nuclear war. The nomination had split the Republican Party, and Johnson knew he could win the election if he played his cards carefully. He did not begin to campaign formally until September, and he refused to give Goldwater a platform by debating with him.

The results satisfied the President's dream. In a landslide election he carried 61 percent of the vote, the highest since President Roosevelt's election in 1936. It was the highlight of Johnson's life. In his own name and as a result of the public's satisfaction with his performance in office following Kennedy's assassination, he had earned the right to be President.

However, being the astute politician he was and despite the Democratic majority in both the House and the Senate, Lyndon knew the honeymoon would not last. Shortly after the election, he called a meeting of congressional liaison officers of various government departments. He explained, "Every day that I'm in office and every day that I push my program, I'll be losing part of my ability to be influential, because that's in the nature of what the President does. He uses up his capital. Something is going to come up, either something like the Vietnam War or something else where I will begin to lose all that I have now."

That speech was an accurate prophecy of what was to come. The issue would be Vietnam, and it would cause a swift decline in his reputation as President.

THE HONEYMOON PERIOD

Kennedy's legacy to Johnson was an excellent Cabinet, and Lyndon was wise enough to continue using the talents of its members after the 1964 election. Most notable of the carryovers were Secretary of State Dean Rusk, Secretary of Defense Robert McNamara, and National Security Advisor McGeorge Bundy. In 1966, Robert Weaver, a black, was appointed to the new cabinet post of secretary of housing and urban development. Combined with a Democratic majority in Congress, the President had a powerful team pushing through the concepts of the Great Society.

During 1964 and the years that followed, the Johnson administration passed many social welfare bills. The Food Stamp Act, passed in 1964, became one of the foundations of Johnson's welfare program. It provided food stamps, to be used as cash for the purchase of groceries, to people at the poverty level of income. In 1965 Medicare was passed; it provided health insurance to people over 65. That same year passage of the Housing and Urban Development Act gave federal rent subsidies to tenants of new housing projects operated by non-profit organizations. The President's interest in education resulted in passage of the Elementary and Secondary Education Act, which gave more than a billion dollars over three years to states to assist education in low-income districts.

The Voting Rights Act of 1965

In March 1965, Martin Luther King, Jr., the black leader, began a march of blacks and whites to Selma, Alabama, to register voters. There they were met by a mounted posse who rode into the marchers and beat them with bullwhips, billy clubs, and cattle prods. Men and women, black and white, were left beaten on the ground or fleeing for their lives. The horrifying scenes were viewed on television all over the country.

Sensing that the time was now ripe, Johnson gave a nationally televised address to Congress urging passage of the

When President Johnson signed the Elementary and Secondary Education Act of 1965, his first teacher, Katherine Deadrich Loney, was at his side. (Lyndon Baines Johnson Library.)

Voting Rights Act. He ended his passionate speech with the slogan of the civil rights movement, "We shall overcome." The bill was passed in August. It did away with literacy tests for voting and authorized the federal government to register voters in those states where less than 50 percent of the voting age population was registered or had voted in November 1964.

Lady Bird's Beautification Bill

A measure dear to Lady Bird (and therefore important to the President) was the Highway Beautification Act. Its purpose was to restrict advertising billboards along interstate highways. Many people were skeptical, and motel and restaurant owners cried that their business would be ruined. But the First Lady stuck to her guns, making carefully prepared speeches to obtain funds and passage of the bill, and in the end, it was passed. Her efforts also succeeded in getting gardens, playgrounds, and parks for the city of Washington and the nation's highways.

LYNDON'S LADIES

As special as the White House years were for the Johnson family, it did present several difficulties. Lyndon, in particular, had little time for Lady Bird and their daughters. Lady Bird, too, had many demands on her time. She was the most active First Lady since Eleanor Roosevelt, and like Eleanor, she was an important political advisor to her husband. The beautification program was Lady Bird's particular contribution to the Johnson administration, but she also helped Lyndon by making speeches around the country on various phases of his antipoverty program.

The hardest part for both Lyndon and Lady Bird was trying to find time to be a family. When Johnson took over as President following Kennedy's assassination, Luci was in high school and Lynda was at the University of Texas. Both girls were always under the watchful eye of the Secret Service men attached to them. Lynda's code name was "Velvet," Luci's was "Venus."

Lynda Johnson, escorted by her father, descends the Grand Staircase of the White House on December 9, 1967, for her wedding in the East Room. The groom was Charles Robb, later to become a senator from Virginia. (Lyndon Baines Johnson Library.)

As Lynda and Luci matured and dated, their romances were closely watched by the Secret Service and gossip columnists. Both young women were courted and wed while in the White House. Luci was married in August 1966 to Pat Nugent, a young man from Wisconsin. Lynda was married in December 1967 to Chuck Robb, a military aide in the U.S. Marines.

One of the great blessings of the White House years was the arrival of two grandchildren, Patrick Lyndon Nugent and Lucinda Desha Robb. However, in the spring of 1968, the family experienced a painful separation when both Chuck Robb and Patrick Nugent left for service in Vietnam. The war had now come home to the Johnson family.

Chapter 9

Vietnam

L yndon Johnson inherited the Vietnam problem from Presidents Kennedy, Eisenhower, and Truman. In 1947, in what came to be known as the Truman Doctrine, Truman had pledged that the United States would resist Communist expansion wherever it occurred around the globe.

In 1954 the French were forced out of that part of Southeast Asia which includes the present-day countries of Cambodia, Laos, and Vietnam. North Vietnam, a more industrialized part of the region, was organized as a Communist state with Ho Chi Minh as its leader. South Vietnam, an agricultural area where most people opposed communism, came under the control of Premier Ngo Dinh Diem. American aid was given to secure a pro-Western type of government in South Vietnam. Ho Chi Minh did not protest this aid because he felt the country would become united once free elections were held. But when Diem sabotaged the free elections, many Ho Chi Minh supporters in South Vietnam formed themselves into a group called the National Liberation Front. This group, popularly known as the Viet Cong, became an underground guerilla force fighting against the South Vietnamese.

President Dwight Eisenhower, in a letter to Diem in 1954, promised to help the South Vietnamese government with economic aid and by training the South Vietnamese Army.

He gave the "Domino Theory" as his reason for providing economic and military aid to South Vietnam. This theory compared Southeast Asia to a set-up row of dominoes. If one domino (one country) was knocked over, the others would fall as well. If South Vietnam fell to communism, so would Laos, Cambodia, and other countries in the region. Under Eisenhower, the first so-called "military advisors" were sent to South Vietnam to help train its troops.

Five months after President Kennedy took office, he sent Lyndon Johnson to assess the situation in South Vietnam. Though Johnson warned about the strong Communist effort and the instability of the South Vietnamese government, Kennedy felt a strong American response was needed, especially after the Communist blockade of Berlin. By the time of Kennedy's death, the number of military personnel in South Vietnam had increased from several hundred in Eisenhower's administration to more than 16,000. Now American military advisors began to fight side by side with the South Vietnamese against the Viet Cong. Just a few weeks before Kennedy's death, however, Diem's government was overthrown and Diem was assassinated.

When President Johnson took over, his attention was first focused on the transfer of government and with domestic affairs. He made a pledge to "see things through" in South Vietnam and went along with the advice of the foreign policy advisors in his Cabinet.

THE GULF OF TONKIN INCIDENT

Three months before the 1964 election, North Vietnamese gunboats allegedly attacked the United States destroyer *Maddox* in the Gulf of Tonkin, a body of water off the mainland of North Vietnam. The President immediately commanded that, if attacked again, the Navy was to retaliate and destroy the enemy ships.

Two days later, on August 4, the North Vietnamese struck again and the Americans were reported to have sunk two enemy boats. (Later sources disclosed that Johnson may have misled the Congress and the public to justify the escalation of the war. Johnson failed to reveal that South Vietnamese patrol boats, assisted by U.S. patrols, had attacked North Vietnamese coastal installations just a few hours before.)

That same evening, Johnson, in a televised broadcast, announced that he had ordered an air strike against North Vietnamese boatyards. The war had now shifted from a defense of South Vietnam to an offensive action in North Vietnamese territory.

Johnson also asked Congress to pass a resolution giving the President authority to "take all necessary measures to repel any armed attack against forces of the United States and to prevent further aggression." The subsequent passage of the Gulf of Tonkin Resolution gave the President full congressional support for any action he might be forced to take. It also served the purpose of proving that Johnson was not, as some Republicans claimed, "soft on Vietnam." The public's positive opinion rating of Johnson rose from 42 percent to 72 percent.

In Congress, the measure passed two votes short of being unanimous. One senator who opposed the resolution was Wayne Morse of Oregon. Morse argued that such a resolution was unconstitutional because it gave the legislature's war-making powers to the President in an undeclared war. It was not until much later that reporters, congressmen, and the public began to question whether the Gulf of Tonkin attack had occurred exactly as the President had presented it or whether he had used the incident in the event he needed backing for future action.

The Viet Cong Attack Pleiku

A month after the 1964 election, the Viet Cong attacked American planes at Bien Hoa airfield. On February 2, National Security Advisor McGeorge Bundy was sent to Saigon, the capital of South Vietnam, to assess the situation. Four days later, the Viet Cong attacked a U.S. military compound at Pleiku, killing nine and wounding 100 Americans.

The President responded immediately. "We have kept our gun over the mantel and our shells in the cupboard for a long time now. . . . They are killing our men while they sleep in the night." With that, he ordered the United States Air Force to bomb North Vietnamese territory.

When Bundy returned, his report left little doubt that the time for action was at hand. The report recommended as the most promising course of action a policy of "graduated and continuing reprisal." Two weeks after Pleiku, the new U.S. commander in Vietnam, General William Westmoreland, requested troops to defend the bases from which the bombing raids would be flown. Now the war began in earnest despite the fact that Bundy's report also stated that U.S. actions should not "represent any intent to wage an offensive war."

A word of warning also came from General Maxwell Taylor, the U.S. ambassador in Saigon. He noted that American Marines were neither trained nor equipped for jungle warfare, that they would not be able to tell the difference between a friendly Vietnamese peasant and a Viet Cong guerrilla, and he predicted that they would fail just as the French had.

Taylor's warnings were ignored. The first bombers streamed north and the war in Vietnam became the President's personal war. Johnson had not started it nor could he win it. Eventually, the war would destroy what he had worked hardest to achieve—a good reputation.

SEND IN THE TROOPS

By April 1965 Westmoreland conceded that the air war in the North would not stop a Viet Cong victory in the South. He then asked for 90,000 more troops to hold four coastal areas. In June, another South Vietnamese government fell, and its army seemed on the verge of defeat. General Westmoreland pointed to the chaos as proof that more troops were needed. He asked for and received permission to begin "search and destroy" operations. The goal of such operations was to go out to the villages, seek out Viet Cong hiding or operating there, and destroy them.

The war witnessed atrocities from the beginning, with both sides assassinating, terrorizing, and torturing civilians and soldiers. When American troops saw their comrades wounded or killed by Viet Cong who often looked like innocent peasants, they became frustrated and enraged. How was one to know who was an innocent civilian and who was a Viet Cong guerrilla? General Maxwell Taylor's warning was coming true.

The Tet Offensive

By the fall of 1967, however, things seemed to be improving. Because more of South Vietnam appeared to be free of enemy control, the President was elated at the turn of events. But in the early hours of the morning on January 31, 1968, the day of the Vietnam New Year, called Tet, the North Vietnamese and the Viet Cong coordinated a countrywide attack. They succeeded in capturing several sections of Saigon as well as several of the major cities in the country. It devastated much of South Vietnam. Though much of the area was later recaptured, the Tet offensive proved to be a terrible blow to the morale of the American soldiers.

THE WAR AT HOME

Lyndon Johnson was faced with several dilemmas at home. He wanted to win in Vietnam, but he did not want to make an open, honest declaration of war. He wanted to spend money on soldiers and equipment, but he also wanted his social programs to be adequately funded. He could not do both without raising taxes or creating inflation.

Johnson wanted to appear as a peacemaker, trying several times to make overtures to Ho Chi Minh. However, he was not willing to give the Viet Cong a role in a peacetime South Vietnamese government, as Ho Chi Minh insisted. Peace negotiations started by Johnson would eventually succeed, but not during his presidency.

The Television War

Vietnam became the first televised war. As more and more Americans landed there, so did the number of television and newspaper reporters. For the first time, on-the-spot reporters and cameramen began to see and report the bombing of civilian populations. Such scenes as a captured and unarmed Viet Cong soldier being shot in the head by a South Vietnamese officer or a naked little girl running down a country lane screaming from the burns on her body left their imprint on the American conscience. Many Americans were also horrified by seeing the scorched, dead land left by the use of 2-4D (Agent Orange), a chemical sprayed from planes that destroyed all plant life.

Student Protests and Riots

The 1960s also saw the beginning of a social and cultural revolution in the United States because of the war in Vietnam. The civil rights movement and the new civil rights laws had raised the hopes and aspirations of blacks and other minority groups in the country. But because men who were going to college were originally exempt from the draft, proportionately more blacks and disadvantaged young men were serving in Vietnam. This led to a growing resentment between blacks and whites, and between the poor and the privileged.

Criticism of the war began with the nation's young people. By the fall of 1965, as the call for men increased, students at college campuses all over the country began protest marches, made antiwar speeches, and demonstrated their anger by sit-ins in colleges and government buildings. Some students burned their draft cards; others fled the country to avoid the draft. As criticism of the war escalated, it began to include Democratic congressmen, peace demonstrators, and newspaper columnists.

Even the President's daughter, Luci, could hear these protests from her bedroom in the White House as demonstrators shouted, "Hey, hey, L.B.J., how many kids did you kill today?" She once sat with her father while the news report on television told of the latest fatalities. Later, she recalled, "It was as if you were looking at a man who had a knife thrust into the pit of his stomach and turned over and over. He just physically looked like he was in agony."

The war was taking its toll on Lyndon Johnson. Late at night, dressed in pajamas and slippers, the President would slip downstairs to the Situation Room of the White House to read the latest reports. He had to know the number of dead, the number of planes lost, the villages that were captured. He wanted to be personally involved in all decisions concerning the war.

Once, in a staff meeting, Johnson described his feelings. "Vietnam is like being in a plane without a parachute when all the engines go out. If you jump, you'll probably be killed, and if you stay in there you'll crash, and probably burn. That's what it is." He could not win and he could not back down.

The deep lines etched into the President's face reflect his anguish over a new Vietnam policy, just before a speech on the subject on March 31, 1968. At his right sits Vice-President Hubert Humphrey. (Lyndon Baines Johnson Library.)

The Credibility Gap

President Johnson tried to win the support of the media — newspapers, magazines, radio, and television — but his efforts failed because he was less than honest with the American public. He would play down the costs of the war and the number of casualties as well as the number of troops he had secretly committed to Westmoreland. He was reluctant to reveal or discuss budgets and would exaggerate any military victories.

Being known for his ability to manipulate the Senate did not help Johnson's reputation with the press and the public. The term "credibility gap" came to describe a growing distrust of the government by many Americans. It began to be used as another way of accusing government officials, including the President, of not telling the truth in their statements about Vietnam. Had the public known the whole truth about the war, it might have affected people's opinions and the decisions made by Congress. In time, the credibility gap began to spill over into other areas of government, with a growing distrust of administration officials.

One result of Johnson's "undeclared war" and the credibility gap was the War Powers Act. In 1973, over President Nixon's veto, Congress passed a bill that placed strict limits on the President's ability to ever again wage an undeclared war.

THE BITTER END

By 1968 more than half a million U.S. soldiers were fighting in the jungles and rice paddies of South Vietnam. Before the war ended in January 1973, more than 50,000 Americans would die and many more would suffer permanent physical and psychological injuries for the rest of their lives. Today, North and South Vietnam are unified under a Communist government called the Socialist Republic of Vietnam.

By the spring of 1968, Johnson recognized that the odds for being re-elected were against him. He never did like to fight. A graceful retreat seemed the best alternative. On March 31, 1968, Lyndon Johnson declared that he did not believe he should devote even "an hour or a day" to personal political concerns. He was, therefore, announcing that he would not seek or accept the nomination for another term as President. The final months in office would have several other tragic events in store for the country—and Lyndon Johnson.

Memorial to an Undeclared War

In town squares in quiet southern towns, in parks in bustling cities—all over America—are memorials dedicated to those who fought and died in the service of their country. Some commemorate the Civil War; others honor the dead of World War I or World War II. One such memorial, located in Washington, D.C., receives more visitors each year than any other monument to our nation's history. It honors the almost 58,000 men killed or missing in a war that was never officially declared.

This memorial, the National Vietnam Veterans Memorial, differs from many of the usual war memorials. It is not a statue on a large pedestal. It does not have a slogan or a war cry engraved on its surface. But its utter simplicity says more than any words could. For on the two large black granite walls which make up the memorial are engraved the names of the 57,939 military personnel killed or missing in Vietnam.

Interestingly enough, the memorial was designed by a woman, a young Yale University student named Maya Lin. A national design competition was held, and Ms. Lin's simple V-shaped, solemn, black monument seemed to best express the nation's feelings. The monument significantly has been placed between the Washington Monument and the Lincoln Memorial. Washington was both our first war hero and our first President. Lincoln, the great Civil War President, lost his life as a result of his efforts to save the Union. The Vietnam Memorial is dedicated to those who fought and died in a small country in Asia to maintain the image of the United States as a country willing to aid those people who seek freedom.

Every day, visitors stream by the two black walls looking for the names of fathers, brothers, sons, or deceased friends. Some come to place flowers at the base where a dearly beloved one is remembered. Others come with pencil or crayon and paper to make a rubbing of a name to bring home in remembrance.

Today, the Vietnam Veterans Memorial receives more attention from visitors than any other monument in Washington. Why? Is it because so many of the visitors are themselves veterans of the war or families of the deceased? Does a name on a memorial personalize the loss more than any statue can? Or do the names, row after row, make the price of war more real than any statistics, any statues, any songs?

Chapter **10**

The Road Home

There are certain years in history when one tragic event triggers another; 1968 was such a year. It was Johnson's misfortune to be President at such a time. For 100 years, blacks had been waiting for equality. Now they had a leader, Martin Luther King, Jr., and enough whites aware of black problems that hopes for remedies were kindled and ready to burst forth. On the issue of Vietnam, Johnson saw himself as following the policy of his predecessors to contain the spread of communism. It may have been that in Johnson's characteristically aggressive, overenthusiastic, and pushy way, he demanded too much of the American people: too much legislation, waging an undeclared war, and a draft of soldiers not only reluctant to fight but not believing in or understanding what they were fighting for.

All of these things came together in 1968, a year of riots, assassinations, and burning cities. The young and the disadvantaged were out front in expressing their anger at the Johnson administration.

ASSASSINATIONS

The end of March not only brought Johnson's announcement that he would not seek another term as President. It also brought the news from the U.S. command in South Vietnam that more American lives had already been lost in Vietnam than in the Korean War.

Also at the end of March, Martin Luther King, Jr., was in Memphis, Tennessee, to help a group of striking garbage collectors. On April 4, while standing on the balcony of his motel, he was shot and killed by a bullet from a sniper across the street. The President went on national television within two hours to announce the tragedy. He also contacted black community leaders and asked them to try to help the blacks go through their mourning in a peaceful way. But years of pent-up feelings could no longer be contained.

As the news passed like wildfire through the black communities, violence erupted. The President had to order out federal troops to stop rioting in the capital, Chicago, and Baltimore. Before the explosive anger could be put down, looting, riots, and fires had taken place in 125 cities in 28 states, leaving 45 people dead, half of them in the city of Washington.

Seven days after King's death, Congress passed and President Johnson signed the Civil Rights Act of 1968. This act was the first major step in open housing, making it illegal to discriminate on the basis of color, race, sex, religion, or national origin, in the rental or sale of housing. But the problems of discrimination and the poor were not solved by one act of Congress. In May, the "Poor People's Campaign," planned before King's death, came to the capital. For a month, caravans of blacks, Indians, Mexican-Americans, and Puerto Ricans camped in West Potomac Park. The shanties that they built were an eyesore in the President's beloved city, and it took great patience on his part not to force some action. By the end of June, however, rain and mud had drained the energy of the people's encampment, and they finally left.

Another Kennedy Dies

The nation had barely recovered from the shock and aftereffects of King's death when, on June 6, 1968, an assassin's bullet struck once again. This time the victim was Robert

Kennedy, a candidate for the 1968 presidential election. He had just won the Democratic primaries in both South Dakota and California and was celebrating in Los Angeles when he was slain.

Although the President had been at odds with Robert Kennedy on several occasions, Johnson was visibly upset at the younger man's death. He immediately went on television to share his feelings of shock and dismay with the rest of the country. In addition, he ordered round-the-clock Secret Service protection for all presidential candidates and their families, a practice that still continues.

There was little respite for the tired and emotionally drained President. He was finally forced to raise income taxes by 10 percent to pay for the war in Vietnam. And the peace talks with North Vietnam, begun in Paris in April, dragged on and on. The only bright moment was the signing of the Nuclear Nonproliferation Treaty with 55 other nations on July 1. As Johnson explained, "The nations that do not seek nuclear weapons can be sure that if they need our strong support against some threat of nuclear blackmail then they will have it."

But by now Johnson's popularity had declined to the point where he could not even win an appointment for an old friend. When Chief Justice Earl Warren announced his resignation from the Supreme Court, Johnson immediately nominated his friend, Abe Fortas, for the position. Though Fortas had had no trouble in being appointed as a Supreme Court justice in the early part of Johnson's administration, times had changed. Now the Senate charged Fortas with "cronyism," that he had acted as an advisor to Johnson on such issues as the Civil Rights Bill of 1968 while he was a member of the Court. That action blurred the distinction between the executive and judicial branches of government. When other charges were also brought up, Fortas finally asked that his name be withdrawn. It was another defeat for the President.

THE DEMOCRATIC NATIONAL CONVENTION OF 1968

Johnson did not want to get involved in the early part of the 1968 Democratic National Convention and the selection of a presidential candidate. Instead, he planned to arrive in Chicago towards the end of the convention to celebrate his birthday and get the last hurrahs from his party members. Posters reading "Happy Birthday, Lyndon" were stacked in the basement of the convention hall awaiting his arrival.

But the nightmare of August 27 and 28 deterred Johnson from making the trip. Because of the presence of a large number of antiwar demonstrators, Chicago Mayor Richard Daley had brought the National Guard and federal troops into the city and had erected barbed wire around the convention hall. It was inevitable that violence would break out. The demonstrators shouted slogans and obscenities at the police, and the police retaliated with clubs and beatings, all viewed on television screens. The police even invaded hotels to beat up demonstrators and more than a few innocent bystanders, leaving the door open to charges of police brutality.

Watching the convention commotion on television, the President decided it would not be wise to attend. The Johnson family and a few reporters celebrated the President's 60th birthday at Luci's home in Austin, Texas.

The Election of 1968

Hubert Humphrey, Johnson's Vice-President, received the Democratic nomination despite the challenge of an antiwar group headed by Senator Eugene McCarthy of Minnesota. Eisenhower's Vice-President, Richard Nixon, was the Republican candidate.

The issue of the Vietnam War was a cloud that hung over

Humphrey's campaign. He tried to find a middle ground, to separate himself from Johnson and yet not antagonize the President. Humphrey wavered, not knowing whether to seek Johnson's assistance and not knowing whether Johnson's efforts would hurt or help the Democrats. Hurt by Humphrey's attempts to offer a more "dovish" stand, Johnson did little to help Humphrey's campaign.

Nevertheless, the President hoped that he could help the Democrats by bringing good news about peace negotiations to the American public before election day. He planned a television speech for the evening of October 31, hoping to make an announcement that the bombing of North Vietnam had stopped and that the South Vietnamese had agreed to join the peace talks in Paris. At the last minute, however, the Saigon government found an excuse not to attend. Although Johnson did anounce the bombing halt, it did not change the minds of most Americans. Five days later, Richard Nixon won the election.

WINDING DOWN

The night before leaving the White House, the Johnsons had a party for the White House staff and their families. When the five-piece Marine band played "Hello, Dolly" and everyone began to sing "Hello, Lyndon," the theme song of his 1964 campaign days, there were tears in many eyes.

The next day Richard Nixon was sworn in as the 37th President of the United States. Nixon asked Johnson how he felt when he realized he was no longer President. Lyndon replied, "I no longer had the fear that I was the man that could make the mistake of involving the world in war, that I was no longer the man that would have to carry the terrifying responsibility of protecting the lives of this country and maybe the entire world."

By the evening of Inauguration Day the Johnson family had flown back to the ranch in Texas. It was a pleasant evening as Lyndon and Lady Bird walked around the yard. The luggage was piled high, and there were no aides around to carry their bags. Lady Bird could not help laughing. "The coach has turned back into a pumpkin," she commented, "and the mice have all run away."

Businessman and Rancher

By the time he retired, Lyndon Johnson was the wealthiest former President in American history. His multimillion-dollar holdings included a number of television stations, part of some Texas banks, real estate, and several businesses in Austin. With it all, he never lost his memories of the Great Depression or his desire to make more money. He also continued to enjoy giving lavish gifts.

With time now available to oversee the ranch and his many business interests, Lyndon became much involved in all operations, particularly of the ranch. He met daily with the staff, wanting to know everything from how the irrigation system was working to the number of eggs the hens laid. He was also very involved in choosing the site and design for the Lyndon Baines Johnson Library and the establishment of the Lyndon Baines Johnson School of Public Affairs on the campus of the University of Texas at Austin. He even watched over the attendance figures of his birthplace, just down the road from the ranch. It had become a mecca for visitors, and he checked regularly to see that the entrance fees that were charged were sufficient to maintain the site.

Lyndon also spent much time taping remembrances or talking to writers he had engaged to help him write his memoirs. But when he saw his words on paper, he was furious. "I can't say this," he roared, pointing to a comment about

*The Lyndon Baines Johnson Library and Museum in Austin,
Texas.* (Lyndon Baines Johnson Library.)

Wilbur Mills, then chairman of the House Ways and Means
Committee. "Get it out right now . . . he may be Speaker
of the House someday. . . . Get that vulgar language of mine
out of there. What do you think this is, the tale of a cowboy?
It's a presidential memoir . . . and I've got to come out looking like a statesman, not some backwoods politician."

Johnson eliminated so much of his colorful language and
observations that the published book, *The Vantage Point,* never

truly presented him as he really was. He wanted the book to reflect the dignity of the President, and he was very concerned about what future generations might think of him.

There were times when Lyndon suffered feelings of depression, especially when he realized how the new administration in Washington was cutting back on his Great Society programs. At those times, Lady Bird would try to cheer him up by inviting friends to the ranch and offering to show them films taken during their White House days. But Lyndon usually refused to look at the pictures or would fall asleep.

Johnson visited Washington on only three occasions after his retirement, two being for the funerals of Eisenhower and Truman. President Nixon was gracious to Lyndon, keeping him informed about matters of state and occasionally consulting him, particularly about negotiations on Vietnam. Nixon also invited Johnson to be present at the launching of the Apollo moon mission in Florida. Politically, Johnson did not play any role in the Democratic Party during the 1972 convention or election.

The former President's happiest moments were with his family and particularly his grandchildren. He had more time to play with them than he had had with his daughters when they were young. People also noticed how special the relationship between Lyndon and Lady Bird had become. He waited impatiently for her returns from small trips and greeted her with a loving grin.

The Final Illness

In April 1970 Johnson agreed to meet with reporters and editors from the *Washington Post*. All who were present from that newspaper could not help but notice how he had changed. His hair was much longer and almost completely white. He had suffered severe chest pains a month earlier, and he still looked pale and almost listless. But once he became involved in the discussion, he was once again the old Lyndon, vigorous and commanding as ever and just as persuasive.

Despite all the warnings by his physicians, Johnson refused to follow his diet, began to gain weight, and even resumed smoking. In April 1972 he suffered a massive heart attack. For the last seven months of his life, he endured chronic chest pains, was quite dependent on an oxygen mask, and took heart medicine regularly. Despite all this, he could not resist speaking on civil rights at a symposium held on December 11 and 12 at the L.B.J. Library. He watched most of the proceedings on closed-circuit television in order to conserve his strength, but once in front of the audience, he gave one of his finest speeches.

Among the blacks gathered at the conference was a group who felt that Nixon's actions had set back the civil rights movement. When they demanded time to speak, Johnson insisted that these people had equal rights and should be heard. The speaker for the group concluded with a demand that a structure should be organized to combat injustice in America. To everyone's amazement, Lyndon sprang up the steps and grabbed the microphone to make an impromptu speech. He had always been at his best on such occasions, and that day he overwhelmed his audience. He told funny stories and urged the audience to reason with Congress, Cabinet members, and the President.

"While I can't provide much go-go at this period of my life," he said, "I can provide a lot of hope and dreams and encouragement, and I'll sell a few wormy calves now and then and contribute. Let's watch what's been done . . . and let's say we have just begun, and let's go on." For that one glorious moment, the old Johnson magic was back. The audience crowded the stage to touch him and let him know he was loved.

A month later, on January 23, 1973, Lyndon was alone

at the ranch. Lady Bird had gone to Austin for the day, and he was taking his afternoon rest when he suffered a fatal heart attack. Although he was able to summon his Secret Service men, there was nothing they could do to save him.

A state funeral was held in Washingon. Johnson's casket was placed in the Capitol rotunda—on the same day that headlines proclaimed a cease-fire in Vietnam. He was laid to rest in the family cemetery in the place he loved best, on the banks of the Pedernales River.

A PLACE IN HISTORY

Lyndon Johnson wanted desperately to go down in history not as just a good President, but as a great one. But world events and his bigger-than-life personality, his often "colorful" language, and his unrefined mannerisms often got in the way. He wanted to be known as the Father of the Great Society, but he ended up as the "enemy" to those demonstrators who opposed the Vietnam War. He wanted to be lauded by the press, but he failed to be honest in what he told them, leading to the credibility gap and a national distrust of the federal government. His era ended with inflation and spending that would continue to plague the country for years. A drug culture emerged that was partly the result of the American soldiers' experience in Southeast Asia.

Yet, during Johnson's administration, the United States was transformed in many ways. Sensing that the time was ripe for action on civil rights, he set the country on a course that continues today. His concern for the poor and the disadvantaged raised the consciousness of the nation. That his dream of the Great Society was not realized does not take away from the fact that his ideals were above reproach. The legislation that he called for provided financing for every level of education, payments for medical care for the aged, disabled, and the poor, and the beginning of a conservation effort that would affect our air, water, and natural resources. Science and technology were boosted by his devotion to the space program. Johnson's administration prodded history into new directions.

Lyndon Baines Johnson aimed high, and he gave to the presidency every bit of his natural energy and dedication. No more can be asked of any man.

Bibliography

Bornet, Vaughn Davis. *The Presidency of Lyndon B. Johnson.* Lawrence, Kansas: University of Kansas Press, 1983. A good source of information on Johnson's presidential years. The last chapter does a fine and fair evaluation of Johnson's place in history.

Caro, Robert. *The Years of Lyndon Johnson: The Path To Power.* New York: Alfred A. Knopf, 1982. The first volume of a planned three-volume life of Johnson. It ends in 1944, with Johnson's years as a congressman. The many anecdotes, especially about his early life, help the reader understand what made Lyndon Johnson the master politician he became.

Conkin, Paul. *Big Daddy from the Pedernales.* Boston: Twayne Publishers, 1986. A very complete and well-organized life of Johnson. The book is a first-rate source for the young adult reader.

Evans, Rowland, and Novak, Robert. *Lyndon B. Johnson: The Exercise of Power.* New York: New American Library, 1966. This book was written by two political reporters who were able to observe Johnson during his years in the Senate. In particular, they chronicle the way Johnson used his position as majority leader to become one of the most powerful men in American politics.

Johnson, Lady Bird. *A White House Diary.* New York: Holt, Rinehart and Winston, 1970. During her years in the White House, Lady Bird Johnson kept a diary of her daily life and that of the President. The book gives an intimate view of what life is like for the President as well as the many roles a First Lady plays.

Kearns, Doris. *Lyndon Johnson and the American Dream.* New York: Harper and Row, 1976. The author was one of the writers who tried to help Johnson write his memoirs. Her experiences with this effort and the many personal insights which Johnson shared with her are included in this biography.

Koning, Hans. *Nineteen Sixty-Eight: A Personal Report.* New York: W. W. Norton, 1987. For those who wish to know more about the critical year 1968, this personal memoir may help the reader understand the many areas of conflict with which Johnson was faced.

Lynch, Dudley. *The President from Texas, Lyndon Baines Johnson.* New York: Thomas Y. Crowell, 1975. Written almost as a novel, this book summarizes the main events of Johnson's life.

Mabie, Margaret C. J. *Vietnam, There and Here.* New York: Holt, Rinehart and Winston, 1985. A simple, well-written background of the Vietnam War, with special emphasis on the roles of the Presidents, from Eisenhower, Kennedy, and Johnson to Nixon and Carter.

Miller, Miller. *Lyndon, An Oral Biography.* New York: G. P. Putnam's, 1980. The author of this book spent more than five years listening to the oral history tapes in the L.B.J. Library and interviewing 180 people who knew Lyndon Johnson. Their stories, interwoven with background information about the period, create a fascinating, "you-are-there" experience for the reader.

Mooney, Booth. *The Lyndon Johnson Story.* New York: Farrar, Straus and Co., 1964. Written by a man who worked with L.B.J. for six years, this book covers his life up to the presidency. There is a good introduction by Johnson in which he gives his political philosophy; excerpts from well-known speeches present Johnson's views on a variety of subjects.

Index